Table of Contents

Lives on the Line
Stories from America's *First*–First Responders

....

Lea Harms

&

Emma Lee

While every precaution has been taken in the preparation of this book, the publisher assumes no responsibility for errors or omissions, or for damages resulting from the use of the information contained herein.

LIVES ON THE LINE: STORIES FROM AMERICA'S FIRST–FIRST RESPONDERS

First edition. October 1, 2024.
Copyright © 2024 Lea Harms and Emma Lee.
Written by Lea Harms and Emma Lee.
Edited by Jennifer Hunt.

Dedicated to our greatest treasures in life: Tyler, Maybel & Harper. We love you. Also, for the English teacher, whose red pen graces these pages in spirit.

Caution

The content in this book is largely based on imperfect memory. While some recollections may resemble transcribed emergency calls and radio traffic, it's important to note that these stories are approximations designed to convey our experiences. Additionally, some names and details have been altered to protect the identities of the people involved in sensitive information. Most importantly, as a wise person once said, ***you cannot unsee something***. Similarly, you cannot ***unread*** this book or erase the images it will create in your mind. Please proceed with caution and conduct mental health checks while reading.

Breathe. Fingers unfreeze, please. Thoughts organize. Pulse, slow down! This is a telecommunicator's mantra during a three-minute conversation where life hangs in the balance. Who knew three minutes on the phone would feel like forever? Who knew each phone call could etch eternal scars in my mind and heart? Silent prayers ask for courage, knowledge, and fortitude to get through this call. And the next one. And the next.

When answering an incoming 911 call, no one can predict what is on the other end of the line. Is it a pocket dial? Or juveniles pranking on a disconnected cell phone? Many 911 calls involve someone who simply needs directions. *RIIIIIINNNG.* The high-pitched tone alerts to another incoming call. Is it a loud noise complaint? Is someone calling to sing the national anthem? Forget theatrics, maybe this one is a theft that occurred a week ago? Perhaps this next one is a sleepwalker calling 911? It could even be a cow in the road, an emergency in a different state, or far worse, a completed suicide just discovered. What about a new mother needing help through labor? Shots fired at a local recreation center during broad daylight? Heart attack? Child drowning? School shooting? We have taken each of these calls and many more during a combined eighteen years of experience in emergency services as 911 telecommunicators (the correct term for emergency dispatchers), and like a box of chocolates, "you never know what you are going to get."

ᴠᴠᴠ

My name is Lea Harms. I was a 911 telecommunicator for eight years in a densely populated county nestled inside the Denver metropolitan area. My career in dispatching began on a whim. After earning my master's degree, I had no idea what to do with my life but knew I didn't want to do the same thing every day, and I wanted to help people, so I took my brother-in-law's suggestion and applied for a 911 telecommunicator job. The initial training was brutal and seemingly impossible, but I pushed myself to the limit. Every day I persisted and prayed I could make a difference.

I experienced peaks and valleys throughout my career. I truly became an adult working ten hours a day, oftentimes during weird hours, sitting at a desk talking to all sorts of people who needed police, fire, or medical assistance. Between 911 calls, I answered nonemergency lines as the front-line operator for the sheriff's office. I also was part of the esteemed group of telecommunicators that are cross-trained to speak with law enforcement on the radio, which requires heightened critical thinking skills and intuition with the thin blue line. Every shift required me to manage extremely stressful situations, train new recruits, and counsel my peers. I spent my best moments at the lazy Susan between our consoles, playing cards and sharing laughs with my shift mates. The toughest days intertwined mental health challenges and the realities of new parenthood with the demands of a job where managing crises, like a high school shooting, was just part of the daily grind. Toward the end of my career, I served as a respected communications supervisor, leading my center's 911 education team and playing a pivotal role in advancing the countywide Senior Check-in Program from a pilot to its public launch. This esteemed project consisted of a dedicated volunteer team committed to calling senior citizens living alone for the purposes of friendship and safety.

Looking back on an eight-year career, I recognize how this job slowly changed me. I have felt the effects of PTSD at least nine times in my career, and I continue to live with that emotional baggage. Because I spent so many years on the phone, I now avoid phone conversations. I was accustomed to eating cold food long before my days as a mom—the universe knows when a hungry telecommunicator has warm food and rewards her with an incoming crisis. Yet within all this chaos existed harmony, teamwork, a sense of accomplishment, and pride from the fulfillment of civic duty. My eight years in the emergency communication center produced lasting effects that will forever form my identity.

vvv

My name is Emma Lee. When my sister told me she was in the testing process to become a 911 telecommunicator, I thought she was crazy! I know my sister. She deeply and emotionally connects with the world, and I wondered if she could handle the stress and be happy with this choice. A year later, I could clearly see that she absolutely loved it.

Meanwhile, I was a stay-at-home mom to my son for eighteen months while physically recovering from sepsis, multiple organ failures, and several invasive surgeries. After regaining my strength and finally feeling more like myself, I decided to get back to work. Lea, in love with her job, encouraged me to investigate emergency services. I hemmed and hawed, but after consulting my husband, who was starting his own career in law enforcement as an officer, I decided to go for it. Getting the job would mean shift work, long hours, stress, and a lot of childcare.

I remember feeling nervous as I walked into the CritiCall exam (the standard multitasking test designed to identify appropriate candidates through stressful drills like memory recall, multifunctional dexterity exercises, and resource management). By the time I finished, I thought it was fun! I wanted more. I scored well on the test, and after a challenging interview process, which included some intense questions about how I would react if my husband was injured in the line of duty, I was placed on a short list of candidates. Luckily someone quit a few weeks after my interview process, and I was offered the position. After a debilitating health crisis, I wanted to do the best I could and silence the thoughts of doubt in my head. *I can do this*, I repeatedly told myself.

After two and a half years in a small, rural, western slope town, my husband and I transferred to a bigger Colorado city, where we have worked together for almost eight years. A year after Lea was promoted, I also received a promotion to Communications Supervisor, and I'm still going strong. While Lea may have hung up her dispatch headset, I plan to remain for as long as I can.

vvv

This job sucks you in. We've lived the highs and felt the lows. Every day in the chair was different and exciting, and the stories are absolutely insane. We are often asked, "what is your craziest 911 story?" and when we share an example, the immediate response is "you should write a book!" So here we are—two sisters, vastly different in our personalities, who both fell in love with the same career and are eager to share our experiences. If you are addicted to true crime stories with a side of popcorn and wine, please continue! Buckle up. Hold onto your butts. Gird your loins. What follows are the realities of being an emergency telecommunicator—the good, bad, funny, ugly, heartbreaking—and a vivid glimpse of what it's like to wear the headset of a *first*-first responder.

Welcome to the Jungle

We never imagined a career hype song. However, Guns N' Roses' popular anthem, "Welcome to the Jungle," fits a telecommunicator's job perfectly. The vibe of this song, which highlights the band's first encounter with New York City, accurately introduces the stories that follow. You have been warned (again).

Telecommunicators for 911 work in a PSAP (Public Safety Answering Point), the place where your emergency call is answered.[*] This technology-filled jungle contains multiple stations, each housing several computer screens, keyboards, and mice. Most PSAPs are located within the jurisdiction they serve, often under the same roof as the police department. Larger PSAPs that dispatch for multiple jurisdictions might stand alone in their own dedicated building. Neither of us have worked in one of those centers, thankfully. We can imagine they feel big and sterile and lack the familial bond of working alongside officers. Instead, we were both blessed to rub elbows with our fellow first responders daily. This culture breeds a close-knit environment between telecommunicators and officers; we are truly one big, dysfunctional family. It's common to park in the secured lot, enter the building, and be greeted by officers and other department personnel. A seasoned veteran could always tell if a large-scale incident was happening based on the number of civilian and patrol cars in the parking lot. When the lot was devoid of squad cars but packed with civilian vehicles, something was amiss. Walking up the stairs, we could hear officers laughing with one another in the report–writing room about the last call they took. Loud voices carried past stale pizza in the breakroom as shift briefing began.

Inside the police department is the PSAP, which is a call center on steroids. PSAPs are unique rooms with secure access; only folks with intentional clearance can enter. These quarters are built to sustain the telecommunicators within; many include exclusive bathrooms, locker rooms, beds, and kitchens. Monthly tours are common because of a center's uniqueness. The parade of wide-eyed community groups, scout troops, or new employee tours gets old, but it's a necessary evil to help others understand what this job entails.

A PSAP operates with incredible technology. Each center is equipped with consoles or stations where telecommunicators perform their duties. The size of the center and its staff dictates the number of consoles. For example, Emma's current center has sixteen total consoles with six consoles consistently in use. Lea's center was similar with twelve total consoles, four of which were in constant use. PSAPs are generally equipped with extra consoles to accommodate overflow staffing in the event "The Big One" happens; all hands-on deck!

Each PSAP console setup can vary depending on the department's budget and operating systems. Generally speaking, a telecommunicator station consists of five or six computer monitors with matching keyboards, three or four mice, a set of speakers, a cooling system, a heating system, foot pedals, and a headset jack. The computer monitors simultaneously run an exorbitant amount of software and programs, allowing telecommunicators to multitask into oblivion. Normally, one or two monitors are used to operate the CAD (Computer Aided Dispatch) system. This is a telecommunicator's primary software program that allows them to create and track an event, or "call for service." Within that event, all system users can see the information in real-time. This allows other telecommunicators to add updates, dispatch and track first responder locations, and log all activity associated with that call for service. Included in this software is a map, command line (a prompt field used to execute updates and make changes to the calls for service via predetermined codes and sequences), and other windows a user can manipulate to display information vital to their job function. Because we answered calls and worked the radio, our CADs were set up similarly with a prominent map and multiple command lines, as well as several open windows that showed pending calls for service (events with no first responder dispatched) and assigned calls for service (events with a first responder dispatched). We also had a separate window that displayed officer status: who is on duty, what they are doing, where they are, and how long they have been there.

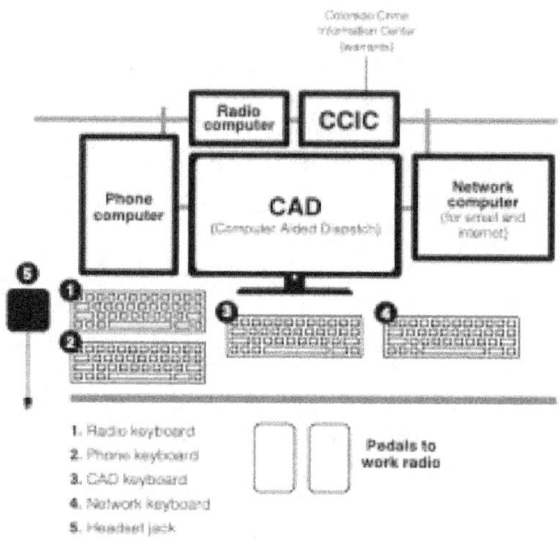

An example of a 911 telecommunicator console

• • • •

ASIDE FROM CAD, AN additional monitor on the console is used strictly for internet access—a vital tool for both training and live events. Another monitor is dedicated to the radio, which we use to communicate with first responders. Most radio software is provided by Motorola. When the program is launched, it displays fifty different radio channels, each labeled so a telecommunicator can distinguish one from the others. To select a radio channel, a user simply hovers over the blue box and clicks it. The selection will light up white, indicating that the channel's traffic is now being exclusively fed to the telecommunicator's headset. A telecommunicator always clicks or "selects" the primary channel they are assigned to monitor, but they may need to "turn up" or listen to other channels for awareness or staffing (i.e., if a coworker takes a bathroom break). In order to monitor multiple channels, a telecommunicator finds the secondary channel and uses the volume slider to turn up that selection. "Radio traffic" (any talking on that channel) will now feed out of the console speakers. It's probable that a telecommunicator in this situation will have simultaneous traffic on channels that they have selected and are monitoring through speakers. Telecommunicators are highly trained to keep up and listen to multiple feeds at the same time. After all, someone's life depends on it.

Our favorite radio extension is the foot pedal. The foot pedal, a heavy mechanism connected to the radio computer, allows a telecommunicator to "transmit" or talk on the selected radio channel without having to use the mouse or keyboard. This piece of equipment is responsible for high-level, multifunctional dexterity. Telecommunicators can use their feet to talk on the radio while keeping their hands free to type notes into the CAD—efficiency at its finest and a telecommunicator's bread and butter. All those years of piano lessons finally came in handy!

Like the radio computer, the last two monitors are strictly dedicated to phone software, which handles the incoming 911 and nonemergency calls. The phone program integrates approximately twelve nonemergency and twelve emergency lines that can ring simultaneously. Nonemergency lines and 911 lines have different ring tones so a telecommunicator can differentiate an incoming line. When all these lines are in use, indicating heavy phone traffic for a large-scale incident, the overflow calls spill into a backup agency's call queue for triage. There are no answering machines in 911. For reference, larger PSAPs average 550 inbound calls in a twenty-four–hour period. On top of having the responsibility to answer multiple calls at a time, telecommunicators must abide by a NENA (National Emergency Number Association) standard, which states "ninety percent of all 9-1-1 calls arriving at the Public Safety Answering Point (PSAP) shall be answered within fifteen seconds. Ninety-five percent of all 9-1-1 calls should be answered within twenty seconds."[1] The phone software configurations are largely responsible for aiding telecommunicators in achieving these high standards. Without the ability to answer, transmit, disconnect, or transfer calls with a click of a mouse or touch of a key, we would be lost.

Each PSAP phone can be individually programmed with a Rolodex of information, including department numbers and frequently used numbers, for quick transfers and references. The phone also has a mapping system that can alert a telecommunicator to a 911 caller's general location. Accuracy depends on the caller's phone hardware, software, calling plan, and proximity to cellular towers. The phone system and CAD system are linked through interfaces, allowing these two programs to talk to each other. For example, when a 911 call is answered by a telecommunicator, the CAD program automatically starts an event window with pre-populated initial location data from the phone. All this saves precious seconds for efficiency, lowers margins for error, and produces faster dispatching times.

Connected to these many monitors are three or four computer mice. One mouse controls the CAD system, another mouse only works on the phone, another is exclusive to the radio, and the last one is for the internet-only computer. If the mice are not in the right spot or the telecommunicator accidentally grabs the wrong one, they can find themselves completely discombobulated. Watching a new trainee on the console for the first time is comical—they constantly fumble, using the wrong mouse for the wrong screen. Seasoned telecommunicators have trained hands that grab the right mouse at the right time for the right action without looking.

And what connects all of this chaos? Cords on cords on more cords. So many cords magically connect the radio, phone, and CAD together into a remote fob base that clicks into a headset and then clips onto the telecommunicator, who wears this base like a badge of honor.

Now that you are familiar with the equipment a telecommunicator works with daily, allow us to introduce you to basic job functions. A telecommunicator can either work the phones, triaging incoming emergency and nonemergency lines, or be cross-trained to work both phones and radios. We are the latter and perform both duties. Oftentimes in a dispatching center, telecommunicators use multiple radio channels to communicate with first responders. It is standard to have at least two radio channels, Channel One and Channel Two.

Channel One, often referred to as "Primary," is the main dispatching radio. The Channel One telecommunicator communicates exclusively with first responders. They utilize critical thinking skills to triage the incoming calls for service entered by call takers into the CAD program. Assessment tools for proper dispatching include policy and procedures, call types, location, and officer availability. *Is this a threat to life or property? Is there a victim involved? When did this happen? Is a suspect still on scene?* These are just a few of the pertinent questions to consider in a matter of seconds. Using these tools, Channel One telecommunicators dispatch first responders, air pertinent information and updates, track unit locations, and help units assigned to calls with ancillary requests that a call for service may warrant. Channel One is a lot.

If assigned to Channel One, the telecommunicator's attention is focused solely on communication with first responders via the radio. Safety is the main priority: a missed or inaudible transmission could have dire consequences. Great telecommunicators have amazing "radio ears" that can decipher the mumbles of incoherent officers and the nonverbal cues and voice intonation that indicate trouble for a first responder. In high-stakes situations where total control of the radio is needed for responder clarification and welfare, Channel One initiates emergency traffic—no interruptions, sole focus on the single call. Situations that warrant emergency traffic include a pursuit, a physical fight, clearing a burglarized business, or pulling over a stolen vehicle.

Every PSAP is different and may have ancillary radio channels that require 24/7 monitoring in addition to Channel One, such as a channel for the fire units, or Channel Two (a.k.a., a data channel). Channel Two telecommunicators query national and state identification information provided by first responders to confirm valid driver status, outstanding warrants, protection and probation orders, as well as stolen property status. The Channel Two telecommunicator is also solely responsible for entering data into the state and national system via the NCIC (National Crime Information Center) terminal for stolen cars, license plates, missing persons, etc. In addition to these crucial responsibilities, Channel Two operators call for assistance from secondary responders like tows trucks, victim advocates, or the coroner. Policy and procedure dictate when Channel One initiates emergency traffic, all other radio traffic moves to Channel Two. There is no harder task in the center than working on Channel Two when Channel One is on emergency. None. Channel Two in this situation is like Grand Central Station during rush hour. Depending on PSAP busyness, this telecommunicator may even have to answer the phone too.

Overall, the procedures on Channels One and Two are very different. While Channel Two is concrete and logical, Channel One is very fluid and situation dependent. In general, telecommunicators learn to prefer one or the other depending on their personality, skill, and comfort level.

vvv

Fresh coffee brews, and the aroma awakens a soul running on empty. The news channel simmers on the breakroom TV. As the horizon chases away the last note of daylight, a telecommunicator fills a water bottle and takes the lonely walk to the console, ready for another shift. Donning the headset worn hundreds of times, the telecommunicator leisurely swings the end of the lifeless cord as it playfully whips through the air. Soon the end of that headset will bond them to tragedy, brokenness, and the sins of this world. Their free hand reaches to pick up the remote base that charges silently and waits for connection. Plucking the base from its charger with a swift motion—*clip!*—telecommunicator and console are united. The telecommunicator sighs and straps the remote base to a belt loop. Now every call and all radio traffic will come through the headset—loud and clear, no escape. Every day is unknown. They ease into the seat, five screens staring back menacingly, and the thin gold line is ready to fight another day.

An Angel

Lea

Walking back to the dispatch floor after a restroom break, I paused to stare at the shadow box gifted to us by the Newtown telecommunicators who handled the Sandy Hook Elementary School shooting. Transfixed by this gesture of kindness, I remembered that there are telecommunicators on the other side of the country who share common pain and trauma from horrific incidents. They understand my anguish. Something unspeakable.

The shadow box still graces the main entrance to dispatch. Inside the box is a simple display. An angel, holding a star in her right hand, floats in a sea of shimmery gold fabric surrounded by twenty-six additional gold stars. Among the stars is a heartfelt note of condolence. The stars represent the twenty kids and six teachers who were lost in the Sandy Hook shooting; the angel depicts the young life we lost in our high school shooting. The gold fabric mimics the "thin gold line" that represents all telecommunicators, much like the "thin blue line" for police. I do not wish to share the commonality of tragedy with Newtown. I do not wish to have these memories. Alarmingly more and more centers are experiencing this pain across the country—school shootings are an evil epidemic that cause immeasurable pain. Although I was not personally connected to anyone involved on December 13th, I cried, screamed, and grieved for those students and parents. Senseless violence stole so much innocence that day. Mine included.

I vividly remember that cold Friday morning. Friday mornings during the winter months were normally mellow. Strangely we had a rollover crash that morning and other calls that pierced the typical cadence. I had completed my six months of training a couple of weeks earlier. I was a beaming new graduate standing on shaky feet, placed on the most senior dispatching team. I loved working with them. Two had taught me during different phases of the grueling training program, so their working styles and habits were familiar to me. Everyone worked together and anticipated needs, helping without being asked. But at the same time, we understood that we were expected to show up and work competently. Don't slack. Bring your A-game. If you ask too many questions, you will get blank stares and a dissertation about which day in training covered that information. Low tolerance for mistakes.

That morning, I was assigned to answer phones. As a new trainee on a relief shift, I hardly ever got a radio—a premium spot, like front-row seats at a Lakers game. Radio positions are highly coveted in emergency communication centers because talking to first responders beats talking to the public any day. Our center has only two radio channels to continuously monitor. While some teams frequently rotated, this team preferred a more consistent lineup. I didn't mind because I was still green and hadn't yet developed my "radio ear." I was halfway into my new book when lunch breaks started—the day was passing quickly. My coworker returned from his break, relieving another to begin her break. Normal stuff. All routine.

At 12:32 pm, the room accelerated from zero to 500. With only three telecommunicators staffed on consoles, I answered the first emergency call. As I clicked into the line, I noticed twelve additional calls fill the queue. Every emergency phone line was full. *What has happened?* A flood of calls typically indicates an inundated area PSAP rerouting calls to a backup center. As soon as I picked up the first line, however, I instantly knew this was not the case. My first caller, out of breath, was a young male running away from his high school after witnessing a male student barge through the athletic entrance carrying a shotgun. Hearing this, I felt myself beginning to panic and slipping into an out-of-body experience. *Is this happening? Wow, it's happening.*

What felt like five minutes lasted only seconds. I snapped back, my inner voice yelling at me, *Lea, you can do this. Move those fingers! You trained for this. Let's go!* Adrenaline pumping, I madly answered as many emergency calls as I could, triaging each one. *Where are you? Are you injured? Are you safe? Did you see anything? What was he wearing? Where was he last seen? What kind of weapon was it?* Meanwhile, I heard my supervisor behind me, yelling for my coworker to return to the dispatch floor.

"School shooting! There is a school shooting, Anita! Come back!" she hollered. Even after Anita returned, we could not keep up. Calls were coming in faster than we could answer them. Without realizing it, I started answering each 911, "Is this in reference to the school shooting?" attempting to save time.

The first person who said "no" shocked me. His truck had been stolen a day ago. I put him on hold and answered the next call, a female who was outside the school and didn't know what to do. I told her to run to safety, then disconnected to move on to the next poor soul. Even though my training was extensive and robust, it did not cover what to say during a school shooting. This was outside the scope of anything I had learned. I didn't have a firm grasp of the totality of the situation, and I was new. I didn't know what to tell these poor kids who were terrified and asking for advice. "Run to safety!" was all I could manage. In hindsight, *run* is a perfectly acceptable answer, according to the FBI. **Run. Hide. Fight** are the three recommended options in an active threat scenario.

The next 911 call was transferred from an agency an hour away. A soft-spoken grandma described receiving texts from her grandson about someone who was shooting in his school. She was petrified. I told her we were working on an active incident and didn't have any more information. She started to sob. Helplessly, I disconnected the call and left her to cry alone, knowing I didn't have the luxury to comfort her. I couldn't take valuable time reassuring her because I had to answer the next call and collect more information. Brutal reality dictated that I must move on.

Looking back, I feel fortunate that every person I talked to made it outside the school. My coworker Anita had spoken with two whispering RPs (reporting parties), terrified as they hid in their classrooms. She stayed on the phone with another student intermittently for an hour using the emergency line to connect the student to their parents for heartfelt goodbye messages. I cannot imagine my response if I had answered these emotional 911 calls or had been assigned to the main radio. The radio traffic was sheer chaos, and as a new telecommunicator, I would never have been able to keep up with the onslaught of transmissions. By divine design, not coincidence, everyone was exactly where they needed to be. God enabled me to answer calls like a machine and gather information from safe reporting parties. I answered and processed as many calls as I could, trying to get the most relevant information.

After twenty minutes, I checked the call notes. The suspect was dead. Self-inflicted GSW (gunshot wound), in the library. Before killing himself, he had thrown a Molotov cocktail and started a small fire. The notes were messy, but I deciphered medical requests for two injured students in addition to the suspect. I took a small breath with that knowledge. But the calls continued. News organizations, from local stations to Al Jazeera, were hungry for updates. Many concerned loved ones from all over the state flooded our phone lines. In addition to the incoming calls, the team and I began making outgoing calls requesting resources from the SWAT team, command staff, investigators, school security, school maintenance, victim's advocates, and the crime lab. The list was endless.

Be-ooop be-ooop be-ooop be-ooop be-ooop pierced through every radio transmission.

"Can someone please call school security and get that damn fire alarm turned off? I can't hear these guys and they can't hear each other!" my supervisor, working the main radio, snarled through gritted teeth. Electrified nerve endings overruled civility and manners.

"I'll do it!" I said confidently, with no idea where to start with this request. I fought to find numbers; my attention was constantly rerouted by incoming phone lines before accomplishing the task twenty minutes later. At this point, my adrenaline began to wane, my eyes were heavy, and my body felt like it had been to war. Nowhere even close to being done, everyone soldiered on in complete synergy.

Our team worked for thirteen hours that day, answering and making calls until our words didn't make sense. The activity level in the center remained fervent; despite this, management knew our team needed to be dismissed. Thankful for the reprieve, I stumbled to my locker to collect my personal items. I reached for my phone and saw voicemails and texts from family and friends, all asking me if I was on duty and if I was OK.

I wasn't OK. I was numb.

As we left the center, we received official confirmation that only one student had been shot—in the face at point-blank range—and she was in critical condition in the ICU. Her prognosis was not good. We thought another student had been injured, but after further investigation, we discovered she was in shock and in unfortunate close range with the gravely injured student. The shooter was dead by his own doing. I prayed for all the families, knowing there was widespread hurt and loss of innocence on this day.

I went home and showered, feeling the need to wash the world away, then I sat on my bathroom floor and cried. *Am I cut out for this job? Could I have done more?* I whispered desperate prayers and begged for comfort, my soul gently and momentarily relieved. Conversations with my older sister in Florida and a member of the peer support staff helped me process my thoughts, but I still struggled to comprehend what happened.

The next day, I returned to the center for my last scheduled shift of the week. It was torturous. My brain had not processed the events of the previous day, and I stared at the mutinous clock after every call, begging for time to speed up. Thankfully, department policy changed after this incident, citing that any team working a large-scale incident, such as an officer-involved shooting or school shooting, has the following day off.

A week later I attended the incident debrief, a newer practice where a psychologist hosts a talk therapy session for those impacted. The science behind this powerful practice has shown that verbally processing a traumatic event and the associated emotions can help move those emotions from the brain's processing center to the memory region. The room was packed for the school shooting debrief. Each department, ranging from the first officers on scene to the crime lab documenting and cleaning up the aftermath, offered their perspectives. I found it most beneficial to hear the entire story and start the emotional healing process. In addition to this session, our team was provided an intimate "dispatch only" debriefing session, which was more impactful. We emptied an entire box of tissues during that raw hour as my teammates shared their experiences, stories, and memories. We discussed the radio traffic, the whispered phone calls, the loss of a beloved student, our actions, what people said we could have done better, how we were doing, and if we were sleeping. It dawned on me that I was witnessing three of the toughest, most long-standing telecommunicators in the center, broken. The four of us passed around the box of tissues multiple times until it had nothing left to give, much like our team.

A few weeks later when the Critical Incident Response Team (CIRT) published their report, we slowly started piecing together the puzzle. The school resource officer (SRO) was in the cafeteria when he heard a maintenance worker on the school radio talking animatedly in Spanish. Without fluent understanding of the foreign words being spoken, the deputy recognized the tone and a single request: "lockdown." This captured his attention, and his hand instinctively cradled his sidearm. As the maintenance man translated his requests to English, the SRO got additional information about a disturbance in the athletic entrance, necessitating the lockdown. He sprinted in that direction, gun drawn. While running, he radioed over the main channel that the school was going into lockdown, and that he was investigating why. Overhearing this information, a nearby SRO at a middle school and a precinct car both called en route to help with the unknown situation. These transmissions happened simultaneously with the first calls into the 911 center. Important help had a head start thanks to the communication of a school maintenance employee. 911 callers had confirmed the worst: a shooting. The SRO also radioed he heard gunfire inside the school as he approached the athletic entrance. After this information was aired, multiple deputies called en route to assist, and the radio was overwhelmed by responders heading that way, lights flashing and sirens blaring.

Because of their proximity, three deputies arrived at the school within seconds. They quickly gathered at the end of the athletic hallway and established a three-man contact team. The fourth deputy was charged with the rescue effort of a gravely injured student just inside the entrance. All heroes. They walked through the valley of the shadow of death, fearing no evil. The three-man contact team quickly marched down the hallway, weapons drawn in search of the gunman. Clued into his location by screams and a path of destruction, they exploded into the library with little regard for their own lives. Their only goal was to eliminate the threat.

I believe that the shooter knew this. I think he sensed that he didn't have time. His plan did not go as he expected. Feeling the pressure, he decided to end his life before he was confronted. The three deputies located him in a corner of the library, crumpled over with a self-inflicted gunshot wound. The terror was over in just eighty seconds. Even though this conflict was deemed "successful," it doesn't feel like success knowing what happened to the young woman who was murdered. Despite all the things that went right, we still lost her. The day was not as "successful" as we had hoped.

Even now, years later, I carry a small token on me at all times, a high school challenge coin. On one side the school mascot stares bravely at me, on the other side are the initials of the student who went to heaven that day. Both serve as reminders that life is precious. Much like the two-sided coin, this was a two-sided day—heartbreak and heroism.

Emma

Wen applying for dispatch jobs, the interviewer always asks the same question. Are you bothered by not getting closure on calls? How would you deal with that? Telecommunicators often conclude their calls without getting the whole story, even if we are the last person to hear the caller's voice. Everyone answers "no" to this question because they do not always know what they are signing up for, but only after it happens does one know the effects of the post-call information void. Not knowing the result of calls slowly wears on a telecommunicator, and it is an unfortunate reality of the job. Most officers and paramedics are sensitive to this and try to follow up with the telecommunicator to give some closure, but this isn't always the case.

vvv

"911, what is the address of the emergency?"

My ear was greeted with rustling noises—something all telecommunicators have heard thousands of times. The skill is discerning whether these rustling noises are a pocket dial—a phone calling 911 in someone's pants—or a true emergency. Pocket dials (a.k.a., "butt dials") sound like people going about their daily lives, walking, talking, and listening to music. True emergencies sound like grunting, yelling, and people pushing buttons in response to questions. True emergencies also give a telecommunicator gut feelings they can't ignore—an instinct confirming something is wrong. Lea affectionately refers to these feelings as "spidey senses."

"Hello? This is 911; do you have an emergency?" I called out again.

More rustling. I thought this could be a pocket dial, but I stayed on the line a little longer. Assessing my phone screen, I deduced the call was coming from a landline. Per policy, a 911 hang-up from a landline requires a call for service to the address associated with the phone number. Oddly, this call was coming from the mall in town.

"Hello? Do you have an emergency?" I asked again, irritation in my tone. The caller grunted in response.

"Sir, if you have an emergency, you need to speak to me!" I tried again.

The person at the end of the line was trying to talk to me, but I couldn't understand his words. Goosebumps covered my arms, and I knew something was wrong.

"Sir, are you in the maintenance hall at the mall?" I asked for confirmation of the location displayed on my phone screen.

"Yes," he said feebly, and my chest surged with joy. My spidey sense had not failed me.

"OK, I'm sending you help. I'm not going to get off the phone until they find you, OK? I'm not going to let you go. We will find you." I tried to soothe him with the confidence that help was on the way.

Realizing the situation and continuing to trust my gut, I sent a medical response without launching the medical questioning protocol, which wasn't going to help in this situation anyway because of his state. I wanted to reserve any strength he had to answer location questions.

Are you by yourself? What is your name? How do we get to your office? These questions attempted to locate the needle in the haystack of the mall. With garbled speech, he was able to answer some, but not all, offering me very vague directions. I kept assuring him we were on the way, and we wouldn't stop until he was found. During our conversation, I heard a noise that resembled a collapse. I yelled across the room to let my fire teammate know, and she relayed everything directly to the fire crew.

Shortly after this, the firefighters found him, and my partner and I released a collective sigh of relief. We listened in as they started protocol for a stroke and requested a timestamp; effective treatment for a stroke requires documentation the moment symptoms are noticed. If strokes are caught quickly, a patient can be saved without many adverse side effects.

The fire and ambulance rushed him to the hospital. Afterward, the fire captain called me and said I gave him the best possible shot of surviving. That was my only consolation that day. I know nothing else about this man's story or what happened when he got to the hospital. I'm one who doesn't always need or want follow-up, but this story lingers in my mind. Perhaps he made a full recovery since it was caught immediately, but perhaps not. I will likely never know.

Lea

Do you ever look at your family and think, *how am I related to you?* We don't look alike. We don't think alike. We don't behave alike. Unlike my older sister—whom I look like, sound like, and share the same birthmark—Emma and I are very different. We have stuff in common and have always shared a special bond (that may or may not have involved long drives after school listening to music on or off the front lawn—sorry, Dad!). But at our core, we are opposites. Nothing made this clearer to Emma and me than sharing the same profession.

My agency hired me in 2013. I had applied many times to multiple agencies across the metro area. I failed the test over here, messed up the interview over there, or was eliminated from the applicant pool for one reason or another. Finally, a recruiter took a second chance on me. I accepted the job with determination to succeed, despite sentiments shared by my closest confidants, including my mother.

"Lea, do you really think you can handle *that*?" she said with her motherly tone. Her question still rings in my ear.

"Yeah, I really do," I said confidently, but inside I was shaking. I am an emotional person. I cry at commercials. *How the heck am I going to take 911 calls?*

Gumption propelled me into the dispatch center for my first day as a telecommunicator, and it was like walking into Batman's secret lair. The number of keyboards, computer screens, mice, cords, and technology would make Steve Jobs envious. I was very intimidated. *Scared shitless* is probably a better term. *Maybe my mom was right.* Even today, I still hold that determination is the most important telecommunicator trait. Yes, critical thinking, multifunctional dexterity, and clear communication are also necessary, but nothing replaces grit. You must be cut from a courageous cloth in order to survive the training, the horrible calls, and the return to the lion's den every day.

I swallowed the lump in my throat and told myself I wasn't leaving. I was going to do it. The intense training lasted six months, during which I had encountered challenging interactions with seasoned telecommunicators and supervisors. The rigorous environment seemed resistant to change, and telecommunicators were expected to unquestioningly adhere to established methods and authority. One morning I tried to contribute to a discussion during the day shift briefing—if looks could kill, I would have died that day. For many, juggling the intense workload within a grueling environment often leads to high turnover. Remembering my promise to myself, I reported for each shift with a fresh-day attitude.

Six months later, my little sis was looking for a job in her small town. She considered applying as a teller at the local bank, but she didn't think that would fully satisfy her. I told her about dispatch and how I thought she would excel in the fast-paced environment. Knowing her so well, I cited her cool and calm demeanor, driven personality, and healthy emotional detachment. She listened to me (for once), applied, and got the job. I was nervous for her. Remembering what training was like for me, I prayed constantly over her. *Let them see her strength. Give her the fortitude to make it.*

Of course she did, and she joined the ranks as a rockstar telecommunicator. I worked as a police telecommunicator in an extremely populated Denver metro county. She worked in two vastly different regions of Colorado—a remote area of the state and a very urban area—as a police, fire, EMS, and campus security telecommunicator. Different calls. Different styles. Same blood.

Several years later, she came to Colorado's Front Range and started at a new agency in the records department—a brief and very unsatisfying stint. She worked her way back to the dispatch center, and eventually, we were both promoted to supervisors. We supported each other and occasionally talked shop. We bonded and shared stories. We connected on life, work, and kids, and we once again grew as close as we had been before life had taken us in different directions. I especially enjoyed talking with someone without having to explain the lingo or the job. Aside from other coworkers, I had a confidant. Someone who knew what it was like to work a graveyard shift with a baby at home. Someone who knew what it was like to have people yell, curse, and scream at you. Someone who also set their iPhone to military time. Someone who got it.

vvv

In 2019 Emma told me about a fall training course she had registered for. Knowing our mutual interests, she sent me the details.

"Oh wow!" I gasped. "This is training my manager said I needed after my promotion!" I wanted to go badly and was instantly jealous.

I'd heard amazing things about this curriculum. Aimed at teaching first responders critical leadership skills, it is touted as one of the top programs in the state at a very prestigious university. Everyone who graduated had only great things to say. Spoiler alert, I am a total nerd. I love school. This training really excited my geeky side. An abrupt kick from inside my belly awakened me from my daydream and reminded me that the timing was not ideal. My second baby would arrive that summer; the class was scheduled for the same time I would return from maternity leave. Approval of my training request seemed unlikely. Disheartened and a little skeptical, I submitted the training request and left my fate in the hands of my superiors.

A couple of weeks later, I called Emma.

"My class was approved!" I shouted into the phone.

"Oh cool," she remarked with more excitement than normal.

"I am soooo excited. So are you gonna be my roomie?" I asked, but really this was more of a statement.

"Um, sure?" she said hesitantly. "A couple of people from my agency are going, and I may have to room with them. I am not sure about the options," Emma said, peppering logic into my enthusiasm.

"Hrmm, well I am going to reach out to the coordinator and ask if it is possible. If the timing works out, I may still be pumping for the baby at the camp. I'd hate to room with someone I don't know. That could be. . .awkward." I winced thinking about baring my breasts in front of a stranger.

"No doubt. Awkward for me too," she stated.

"Stop it! I'd rather you see my boobs than a random lieutenant from another PD," I said with laughter, but it was anything but a joke.

"Ugh!" she moaned. "You are going to make me do this aren't you?" I could tell she was rolling her eyes.

"I'm emailing them tomorrow!" I said with gusto, ignoring all of her protests.

To my surprise, the school accommodated our request to room together, despite the program policy of pairing unfamiliar classmates together so that everyone meets new people. The coordinator excitedly remarked, "Wow, we have never had sisters before! This will be so fun."

Emma and I chatted excitedly about transportation, packing requirements, and the pre-class homework until we pulled into the retreat center and gasped. We left behind the bustling city for the tranquility of a forested landscape. The crisp fall air and the scent of pine trees surrounded us. Patches of crunchy snow lay resolute, bolstered by the shade of large trees. A stunning view of Pikes Peak, one of Colorado's most gorgeous fourteeners, provided the perfect backdrop for the learning adventure.

When we entered the first session on a perfectly brisk morning, packets of information awaited all of us. The contents of the twenty-plus page document outlined our personality style, interaction with others, as well as our key strengths and weaknesses. It also disclosed our value to the team, blind spots, opposite types, and management tendencies. Every detail was eerily accurate. *Had this team of instructors been following me my whole life? How did they pinpoint my personality type to a T? Was I participating in a Truman-esque reality show?* I looked around the class and saw the entire group plagued with looks of similar consternation. The instructors noticed our discomfort and laughingly explained how they gathered this information from the "Insights Discovery Test" we had filled out prior to attending the retreat. Our results categorized our core truths about self, others, and our organization into four colors. Red was a thinking extrovert. Yellow was an extroverted feeler. Green was an introverted feeler. Blue was a thinking introvert. All these colors illustrate a bevy of varying work styles in organizational leadership and development. The course powerfully highlighted how to use color strengths to guide and understand yourself, your teammates, and your organization. The insight from this amazing class truly changed my life.

What is my color, you ask? You may have already guessed it, but I am sunshine yellow. Bright, bubbly, social, people-person. Quite a rarity in the emergency services field, I was one of two yellows in the entire class. Emma, on the other hand, is a deep blue. Quiet, logical, intense. Polar opposites, in every single way.

One exercise involved mapping our colors, backup colors, and opposite colors in a gym. We all moved around according to our distinction. Every time I moved; I saw my sister's green eyes matching my blue ones from across the room. We never even touched the same quadrant. It took a few hours for the camp attendees to believe we were biological sisters. Soon our opposition was a running joke amongst many. Our experiences at the camp broadcasted our differences, but more importantly provided me the opportunity to deeply reconnect with *my sister.* My sister. No amount of blue or yellow changes the life experiences we share and the connection we have. Yes, during the nighttime activities, she preferred the solitude of our cabin while I socialized in the lodge with my co-campers, beer in hand. However, hearing her voice cheer me on as I maneuvered across the high ropes course and laughing together, knowing we both made it to a standing position on top of the totem pole, reminded me we are more alike than different.

Because of this class, I understand Emma better and found ways I can more effectively demonstrate my love and support. She withdraws into quiet solitude in order to recharge, and her pensive nature allows her to process. As a socializer and talker, I need to remember and honor that. Additionally, in order to address a difficult topic with her, I must approach with logic and facts over emotion. This trip gave me a new respect for who Emma is and how she operates. We revealed our true colors in the Rocky Mountain air, and that is something Cyndi Lauper would be proud of!

Lea

Have you ever had a day that just beat you up, chewed you up, and spit you out? One where the punches just kept coming? I've had several in my career, and one particular day stands out among them all.

I began my second consecutive day working Channel One. As a shift supervisor, I crafted the shift assignments, so no one got stuck working the same position for too long. My motto was always "share the wealth" in order to build skill sets and well-rounded telecommunicators. This particular week presented some staffing challenges, so I worked the main radio for the second day in a row. I didn't mind, though—I liked the action—but this day inundated the center with too much action. Five priority calls came in within twenty minutes: CPR in progress on a choking child, a robbery at Chase Bank, a missing kid, and two fires. Radio traffic gets crazy with one priority call—five back-to-back left me feeling completely out of control. I struggled to keep up with call updates and accurately track deputies. Danger zone!

The first call, a bank teller, reported a female customer who entered the teller line and slyly passed a note across the threshold. The teller unfolded the paper to find these words,

"This is a bank robbery. If you do not comply with my demands, I will hurt you. Give me all the cash in your drawer. No trackers."

The teller complied with the suspect's wishes and called 911 immediately after she left. The suspect headed northbound on foot and soon disappeared; the teller presumed she got in a vehicle. Adhering to Priority One dispatch policy and procedure, I predicated my dispatch with a high-pitched alert tone.

Bop beep bop beep.

"Edward 31 copy, a robbery—just occurred," I aired.

"Go ahead," he replied.

"Robbery just occurred at the Chase Bank, Big Creek and County Line. Again, the Chase Bank at Big Creek and County Line. The female suspect passed a note and left on foot northbound." I aired the facts.

"Copy, en route Code 3." He informed me about his intentions to initiate a lights and sirens response to the bank.

All units on that half of the county began driving toward the incident to assist. Left and right units who had been responding to different calls for service, posted on traffic assignments, or were on breaks cleared their duties to respond. The opportunity to run lights and sirens was a treat for units on the road. A deputy quickly arrived on scene, and I initiated emergency traffic, which forced all other first responders not associated with the bank robbery call to take their transmissions to Channel Two. During this time my Channel Two operator sent a metro-wide BOLO (be on the lookout) bulletin informing nearby jurisdictions about the robbery. Soon, a neighboring agency called and said they also had a note-passer rob a Chase Bank in their city ten minutes earlier. *Super helpful.* The suspect descriptions matched, and the units concluded the female suspect was definitely associated with a car due to the spree timelines. Unfortunately, she was long gone.

Four minutes after my deputy arrived at the bank, he advised he was "Code 4," cop lingo for "I'm OK." He provided more information about the suspect, and my teammates worked hard to update neighboring agencies, including metro transit, with the newest details—including our suspect's polka dot purse! The day you rob a bank is not the day to bring a distinct article of clothing. Not long after, metro transit reported a female on a bus with a polka dot purse. Many units called en route to the next stop on the transit line to confirm this was the suspect. The dispatch center waited with bated breath. A few minutes later, a disappointing result: no positive ID. We rarely catch robbery suspects the same day.

Meanwhile, another priority call dropped in the queue—a choking child in the same area. All my units were occupied with assignments associated to the bank robbery, and I realized I didn't have an available unit for this important call. Thankfully, a dayshift car, nearing the end of her shift, sensed my struggle and offered to respond; I relayed information that the child was turning blue. The RP was the child's father who was trying in vain to dislodge the blockage. Rescue units responded, and several units broke from their existing assignments to respond with lights and sirens to this medical call. I whispered a prayer for the youngster.

I considered taking a break to pee before the medical call units arrived, but the universe had other plans. Another Priority One call blinked in my dispatch queue. As it screamed for attention, I knew my bladder had to wait. I quickly assessed the call, a fire in a very remote area of the county known for country bumpkins, cows, and controlled burns. *Well, at least I have a car for this one! Huzzah!* I sent my available precinct unit—mischief officially managed. The center continued to buzz; rollover calls from another agency reported a bad accident on the highway. Our emergency call queue was full—all twelve lines brimming with concerned callers. Through this chaos, my call takers, all sitting five feet away, attempted to give me verbal updates about our calls for service. I couldn't hear them. I couldn't even hear myself think, let alone hear something from across the room. The intense radio traffic continued, and I was frantically documenting the calls from the investigations unit for the bank robbery while simultaneously tracking multiple deputies' efforts going Code 3 to various calls.

Another priority call dropped. *Ugh, no!* I checked for available deputies and saw I was running thin on units to go to any new calls. Sniffing around, I finally found a unit on a low priority call.

> "Edward 53 can you break and copy a missing juvenile?" I kindly asked.
> "Go ahead," he gruffed, and I relayed the information I had.

It wasn't my favorite call for service—the information came third hand from an RP not on scene. Diluted third-hand information is always hard to work with. In this instance, the information contained frustratingly scant detail. Regardless, my deputy was on the way, and several units adjusted to make themselves available.

With county emergency services stretched thin, I aired the official announcement from command staff that all dayshift patrol units and telecommunicators would be held over to help with the impressive call load. No one would leave on time. This rare circumstance happens occasionally when a large-scale incident—or four—is in play. My queue of stacked-up calls miraculously began disappearing as the dayshift units accepted their mandatory overtime imprisonment. Thankful for the support, I felt my anxiety and OCD wane as the calls in the queue began to evaporate.

With an improving mental state, I received a transmission from a deputy with pertinent information about the missing child. He remembered the address from a similar situation last week. Bitter custody battle. I took his information, transcribed it, and used the address history CAD function to locate a phone number for the kid's dad. Meanwhile, units arrived on scene of the choking child. Rescue transported the unconscious boy to the hospital, and additional police units accompanied them, except for one car that was instructed by the lieutenant to stay on scene and "hold the threshold." I had never heard that phrase, and I filed it away for questions later.

Returning to the missing kid, I saw notes added regarding the custody battle. The unit couldn't reach the dad. Keen to investigate further, my deputy called the school SRO and was discussing the kiddo's whereabouts that day. This call needed no further immediate assistance; I shifted my focus elsewhere. Like a waiter working the busiest dinner rush, I triaged my calls as if they were customers at tables.

Perusing my other call updates, I noticed Channel Two had requested victim's advocates (VAs) meet the parents of the choking four-year-old and staff at the Chase Bank. Victims of crimes have rights in every state; VAs inform them of their rights and advise them of the next steps through the judicial process. The VAs were on their way, and I said a silent prayer of thanks that these incidents didn't occur during a graveyard shift. VAs awakened from a dead sleep and forced to get their bearings for a call response take twice as long. Thankfully, it was a normal Tuesday afternoon.

This reprieve didn't last long as another fire in a remote area of the county dropped into the queue. I scrounged to find units for response. More lights and sirens blared out east. I swallowed hard knowing more units had risked their lives initiating Code 3 responses to calls for service on this Tuesday in November than that entire year. Another call blinked petulantly on my unassigned call list. I saw it was titled "Info," and I knew it was going to be trouble. A telecommunicator uses the "Info" label as a catchall "Hail Mary" when nothing else quite fits. I skimmed through the narrative. A neighboring agency advised there was a possible fire near our shared jurisdictional boundary. This agency advised the possible fire was on our side of the road, and there was a suspicion of arson. Like a hot potato, this call for service landed right in my lap. *Just what I needed.*

"Any car for a possible arson in Precinct 4?" Running low on critical thinking juice, I saw no available units and tossed out the last-resort Channel One calling card. D21, a dayshift unit two precincts over, stepped up for the assignment. I slumped in my chair, elated to know someone was going.

"David 21 be advised suspect is going to be a female walking westbound, wearing sweats," I informed, referring to the arson suspect.

"I copy," D21 said accepting the description.

"Thank you at 1638." I timestamped the transmission.

"Edward 42 I'll be in the area checking the residential streets and business park at the corner of Jolton and Havana," a different unit declared.

"Copy at 1639." The search for the arson subject continued. Time was not on our side. Every second that ticked by decreased the likelihood of finding her in this dense, sinuous area.

"Edward 42 to dispatch," he said with urgency.

"Go ahead," I prompted, fingers ready to record his update. "I'll be out with her, north side of the Palomino business park. Can I get a cover car?" he requested.

"David 21 enroute."

"Copy, thanks David 21 at 1641." I concluded the transmissions relieved that we had at least located one nefarious female suspect.

Two minutes after the cover car arrived on scene, I checked the unit's status.

"We are C4 for now. This suspect is also associated with a male. They fought at the golf course. After the fight, the male started the fire. Can you roll rescue this way for a head lac?" he asked.

"Affirm at 1651," I copied while simultaneously dialing the fire department for assistance assessing the female for injuries.

The deputy also provided a description and direction of travel for the male suspect. Based on the interview with the female, we had airtight domestic violence and harassment charges. Additional units flooded the area attempting to locate the male. *What a strange twist.* This info call was now dubbed the domestic-violence-harassment-arson-fire. Say that five times fast.

Finally, a favorite deputy of mine called out with a male matching the description over a mile away from where the fire started.

"Any car as cover for Edward 61?" I asked, knowing he would likely need a second unit.

"David 61 I can start that way," a unit piped up.

"Thank you, sir, at 1704," I ended.

Soon after some status checks, the male was headed to jail on what I presumed were domestic, harassment, and arson charges. The female was transported to a local hospital, and we requested another VA to meet her there. A busy day for everyone.

At last, I had a moment to breathe, so I checked all the other calls. The fire department beat us to both fires in the eastern part of the county. Knowing they were on scene, I slowed my deputy's response from lights and sirens. I called the fire department for updates and found that one fire had not been located and the other was a controlled burn. With this information, I canceled the response for both of my units entirely. Done.

A deputy working on the missing kiddo call advised me that the dad had picked up his son from school that day. He claimed there was a "communication mix-up" about whose day it was. I rolled my eyes and sent some good vibes to that youngster. He was going to need some thick skin to weather his mom and dad's divorce.

I took a long, slow breath and sat back in my chair. Around me, my team's shoulders came out of their ears. Relief shifted to teasing and telecommunicator banter. One telecommunicator insisted I will never again be allowed on Channel One. This was always my favorite post-apocalyptic PSAP game. *Who is to blame for the crapstorm?* On this day, it was my fault, despite my usual propensity to be the "queen of calm." I blame Tuesday. Tuesday afternoons were statistically the busiest times of the week with the most call volume, rivaling Friday and Saturday nights.

Our dispatch jesting took a sobering pause when the hospital treating the four-year-old boy called for the coroner. The child didn't have a pulse when he was transported from the house, which explained why the scene was to remain secure. Many details connected and shattered my heart as I considered this loss. The center grew quiet as we reflected on the tragic accident that began with a fun post-errand ice cream treat. A swing shift telecommunicator gently relieved me of my Channel One duties for the day. "I've got the radio, Lea," she said confidently.

"Thanks," I said flatly. My fingers used my mouse to deselect out of the radio channel, and I gingerly took off my headset. I was tired. Exhausted. Beat to hell. All my nerve endings were raw. I stood and stretched, painfully aware of that bathroom break I neglected. As I retreated from the dispatch floor, my coworker hollered that the team voted, and I wasn't allowed on Channel One for the rest of the week. I turned to face her with a smile.

"Fine by me!" I shouted.

Lea

I spent roughly half my career working the overnight shift. My first year on graveyards was especially awesome: I was pregnant with my first child, and I had a great supervisor, coworker, and patrol team. We had so much fun while working really hard. Many calls came into our center that provided comic relief to our otherwise serious shifts—some of the most remarkable include a sleepwalker, a drug-induced clown hallucination, and a handful of prank calls that left us in stitches. It's important to note that not all 911 calls are serious. In general, we talk to people on their worst days, but in some moments, God provides hilarity. The humorous calls are just as memorable as the sad ones.

I felt empathy and camaraderie with one sleepwalker. As a little girl—and, admittedly, even now—sleepwalking was a regular occurrence for me. Countless times as a child, I would wake up crying after I had set off the home alarm system trying to exit a locked door while carrying baskets, TV remotes, and other various items collected on my nightly walkabouts. Most recently, I sat up straight in bed and babbled nonsense about a dream, awakening a room of my girlfriends, who were quite amused. On another occasion, my husband recorded me walking around our bed and into the bathroom, unintelligibly and persuasively rambling about going to the bank. In the midst of his interrogation, I gained some clarity and embarrassedly returned to my side of the bed for sleep. When recounting these two situations, I am commonly asked, "Do you remember?" My memory is foggy at best. I'm curious to ask a 911 caller this question myself.

One warm summer night, I was working phones. Vastly different from the dayshift, the nighttime staffing is skeletal and therefore cross-trained and highly skilled at multitasking. A nighttime telecommunicator often listens to two radio channels while also answering the phones. These skills come in handy when your partner needs a restroom break or someone calls in sick and there is no backfill staffing.

A 911 call came in, and I immediately identified it as a landline call from a residence. A landline call to 911 routes directly to the correct PSAP, whereas cell phone calls find the nearest geographic cellular tower and route to the PSAP where that tower is located. The jurisdiction of the tower and the jurisdiction of the emergency may be completely different, which is why telecommunicators transfer amazing amounts of cellular calls. Both parties of a cellphone call become frustrated: callers don't understand why their call is getting transferred, and telecommunicators are equally vexed by technological limitations of the system. This is why it is paramount to be aware of your location when using a cell phone in an emergency! Unlike a cell phone, a landline is magically hardwired and programmed to connect to the correct PSAP. Telecommunicators also send assistance to every 911 hang-up call from a landline; most hang-up calls are accidental or kids playing, but I can think of a dozen times in my career that it wasn't. Landlines save time during an emergency and therefore save lives.

That night as I assessed the phone screen, I knew the exact location of the caller thanks to a landline connection. A male voice, small and quiet, met my ear. I started a call for service in CAD after he didn't respond to my first inquiry.

"Sir, do you need help at the Ohio address?" I asked for the second time, attempting to engage him.

"No, I am at work," he stated, and continued to ramble about Subway. I was unsure if he was referring to the fast-food joint or the transportation method. I tried to clarify, but he was not making any sense. I took a mental step back and put on my thinking cap to assess the facts. It was one o'clock in the morning. I knew he was calling me from inside his house. He was spewing nonsense. Like a lightbulb switching on, I suddenly realized that this poor fellow was asleep! I laughed at my good fortune. This was going to be fun.

Not one to ignore policy and procedure, I continued updating my call for service and noted my suspicion that the caller was sleepwalking. Jordan started the dispatch on Channel One, and I could sense the amused deputy from my seat in the PSAP. I didn't hang up the phone and instead kept the subject engaged, just in case something sinister was going on. His meek voice continued putting random sentences together about Subway and being at work.

I maintained a polite conversation with this sleepyhead while simultaneously anticipating the arrival of my unit.

"Sir, can you please go to the door? I have a deputy who wants to talk to you," I said, watching the map indicate a unit on scene.

"No," he stated matter-of-factly, "I am in the basement and cannot get up the stairs." *Oh boy.*

"Why can't you get up the stairs?" I asked incredulously. To this, he repeatedly mumbled "no" while I heard the deputy loudly announcing his presence at the door.

"Sherriff's office!" could be clearly heard accompanying thunderous knocks at the door. Judging by the clarity of those knocks through the phone, it definitely didn't sound like he was still in the basement! As I pondered how to ask the caller for clarification, the phone went dead. I tried to call back and got a busy signal. Disconnected and off the hook. Sleepyhead must have taken himself back to bed or awakened and didn't understand why the cops were at his front door. Stuff of nightmares for most folks. My deputy cleared the call via the radio with a "no report" disposition. I called him immediately, and we both shared a good laugh about that sleepy man at Subway. My deputy said nothing looked unusual or out of place. Just a man after my own delirious and drowsy heart.

While sleepwalking can create some erratic delusions, drug use can also have the same effect. Our graveyard trio worked a crazy call for service one night that had us all in stitches. I was working Channel Two, while Erin manned phones and Jordan sat at the helm of Channel One. Erin struggled two minutes into a 911 call where a male insisted a clown was harassing him at his house. He repeatedly said he was home alone and was very creeped out by the presence of the clown. Careful questioning and trained telecommunicator spidey senses confirmed this situation was not a ghoulish nightmare.

"Have you been drinking or using any drugs?" Erin asked blankly, attempting to confirm her suspicions.

"Both, but that is not the POINT!" the caller answered emphatically.

"What does the clown look like?" Erin asked, avoiding the argument and attempting to keep the call moving forward.

"Have you ever watched *Britain's Got Talent?*" the caller stated with remarkable clarity.

"No," Erin replied, amused.

The discussion continued, weaving sinuously as the caller tried to describe a clown that resembled a contestant on the show. Through his brain fog, he couldn't remember the name. I noticed Erin's notes mentioned "Puppy the Clown," so I did a quick Google search and identified "Puddles the Clown" as our suspect. I added this information to the call notes with a giggle.

I saw Erin pull up a picture of Puddles at her station and heard her reference his features for verification. The caller affirmed her questions and confirmed that Puddles the Clown was in his house. Jordan attempted to air the information with professionalism, but the deputies' puns, questions, and outlandish commentary made keeping her composure very difficult. As soon as the caller identified Puddles as the suspect, a responding deputy with a keen sense of humor aired a description of the clown. Soon everyone on this patrol team had access to a meme mug shot of the clown for accurate reference. These guys and gals knew how to have a good time with a ridiculous call. As soon as the units arrived on scene, they announced themselves at the door and contacted an occupant. Erin told the panicking caller that help had arrived, and she was going to disconnect. Our stomachs in stitches, we all took deep breaths to compose ourselves. We waited with bated breath for the next status check and details about what was happening on scene. Three minutes felt like an hour.

"Frank 41 and other cars, status?" Jordan asked.

"Code 4," he replied. "In contact with three at the residence, no sign of Puddles the Clown. Can you roll rescue for an eval?" He finished his status update with a telling request.

In the end, our caller was indeed not alone in the home. Although Puddles the Clown was nowhere to be found, a roommate and the caller's brother were fast asleep while our subject took a mushroom trip. Rescue evaluated the subject and deemed him safe to stay home and recover from his drug episode. Here's the lesson, kids: drugs can cause you to imagine creepy clowns in your house, while also bringing you shame and embarrassment as a whole county of telecommunicators and cops laughs at you.

Another good laugh occurred on the night of our prank calls. Someone wanted to mess with us and knew exactly how to do it. Unluckily for me, I was the one on phones that night. The first call came in around one in the morning.

"County communications, this is Lea," I answered the incoming nonemergency line.

"Nick's Pizza here. I'm trying to find out where I should drop off these pizzas you ordered," a male voice stated.

"Uh, I didn't order a pizza," I said, startled. This really threw me off my game. I turned in my chair to look at Jordan and Erin. They peered at me incredulously.

"Is your address street or lane or whatever?" he said, sounding like a California surfer dude.

"What? This is the sheriff's office sir!" I said with frustration.

"Twenty pizzas and some sodas. I just need your address for whatever party you are having," he drawled out, sounding unfazed by my demeanor.

"Sir, I think you have the wrong place. No one here ordered a pizza." I gawked at my keyboard, not sure where to go with this call.

"Where do you live? I need that so I can deliver these and get back to work," he added, interrupting me.

"Guys, no one ordered a pizza, right?" I said, spinning around in my chair. The puzzled look on both Jordan and Erin's faces was proof enough. Hearing me struggle, Jordan clicked into my call to listen in.

"Sir, this is a 911 center. We didn't order a pizza," I stated sternly.

"Look, I don't care. You ordered these pizzas, you gotta pay for them," he said. Jordan immediately started laughing. I gazed at her, missing the punchline and getting even more annoyed.

"Lea, have you never had one of these? It's a prank call! Just hang up!" she giggled, slapping her desk.

I'm sure my face was priceless. Blonde hair got the best of me. As I disconnected, Jordan and Erin laughed at my gullible nature. They swapped stories about saving up money to prank their frenemies on a Friday night. I had nothing to contribute, aghast that these recordings exist.

Two hours later I was assaulted again.

"County communications, this is Lea," I answered the nuisance phone ringing at two thirty a.m., causing us to pause *Sabrina* on Netflix.

"Hello, are you there?" a male said with a thick Indian accent.

"I'm sorry, sir, who are you looking for? This is the sheriff's office," I said, taken aback.

"This is Kerpal," he matter-of-factly stated.

"Kerpal, how can I help you?" I evened my tone to mask my annoyance.

"You can tell me why you kicked my dog today," he blurted.

"I'm sorry? I didn't kick your dog," I said defensively.

"You kicked my dog, I saw you!" he yelled. Although I am no stranger to people yelling at me, this direct accusation was different.

I was stunned and confused. I continued trying to calm the man and assure him he probably had the wrong phone number. His volume continued to escalate, and he kept interrupting me with statements that didn't make sense. Pausing, I took a deep breath and remembered the pizza call. I stayed silent and let the prank script play out. I was rewarded when the call ended saying, "You've been pranked by PrankDial!"

"Guys! I just got another prank call!" I laughed, motioning Jordan and Erin over to listen to the playback. As we listened to the recording, we speculated who could be sending these silly calls. The culprits never revealed themselves, but I suspect a couple of deputies, good friends from the patrol team.

Do I encourage anyone out there to send prank calls to your local PSAP? Never! Prank calls can interrupt vital operations during emergencies, but these calls certainly offered a different perspective showcasing the small joys in telecommunications.

Lea

My eyes were tired, and my brain was fuzzy after another shift had sucked the life out of me. This day had provided nothing particularly crazy except for the sheer volume of things. The sugar crash after eating two donuts may have also played a part, but this day reminded me of a job "requirement" I maintained. I never wanted to do the same things every day. Well, mission accomplished! Sitting in the dispatch hot seat was ever-changing. I used to tell my trainees that you can take a million calls for accidents or theft from motor vehicles but no two will be the same. Every call involves different directions of travel, suspects, time frames, vehicles involved, and reporting parties. This job was always different. And technology was constantly evolving and changing as well. That was precisely what put me over the edge on this day. Computer updates. IT often interrupted our shifts to update our computers and move monitors, and on this particular day, their work alongside some crazy calls made for a day to be remembered!

I set my water down at my station and grabbed my headset. Eager to get to work, I rattled my mouse and saw a different welcome screen glaring at me as the computer responded. Groaning, I remembered that IT did operating system updates the night before. Behind me, the choruses from the we-don't-like-change telecommunicators reflected my sentiments. Everyone complained about issues with their consoles. As the floor supervisor, I had the joy of problem solving and empathizing with cranky telecommunicators. I spent the first hour of the shift sending frantic emails with screenshots to our IT team. After a lot of back and forth, they sent a *lovely* staff member with a sharp attitude and a sloth-like work ethic. After some rough and tumble maneuvers, including a complete uninstall and reinstall of our CAD software, we were all cleared to sign in. My station continued to have other issues, and I spent another hour with my favorite IT employee updating my computer settings and preferences between 911 calls.

After two hours of technology-induced anxiety, I resumed a normal rhythm. I assumed care of Channel One, and a call came in from a neighboring agency via MetroNet, a shared radio channel between Denver metropolitan agencies reserved for quick updates about situations or suspects. They advised that units were following a truck with stolen license plates headed in our direction. A stolen plate generally indicates a stolen vehicle. This agency requested our assistance stopping the vehicle.

"Aurora, I have a deputy en route," I aired.

"Copy, can you all go C3? My officer thinks the truck may be eluding," the Aurora telecommunicator asked.

"I'll step them up. What is an updated location?" I asked.

While listening for the answer on MetroNet, I deftly used my foot pedal hardwired into Channel One to request sergeant approval for an emergent response on the Aurora assist. MetroNet radio traffic blared out of the console speakers while my deputies traffic remained in my ear. I used two keyboards and two mice to switch between computers, software, and screens in a bid to accomplish this communication fluidly. This was no small feat.

Meanwhile, my adrenaline was building. Policy and procedure dictate that in high-stake situations, like pulling over a stolen vehicle, officers initiate a "felony stop" and remove the driver from the vehicle at gunpoint. Additional units for cover are mandatory, and the main channel will initiate emergency traffic (reserving communication on Channel One for officers related to one incident).

"David 61, I'm on scene with Aurora," my deputy aired.

"Channel One is on emergency traffic for David 61. Channel One is on emergency at 1323," I advised, reserving the channel for his radio traffic only. Twenty seconds after airing this, a different unit in a different city on a different call gave me radio traffic.

"Sir, take your traffic to Channel Two!" I barked at him.

Rawr! "Get off my channel, you imbecile!" I muttered under my breath. Then I waited. Impatiently. A minute later my deputy advised he was C4 with two people detained. The same update aired on MetroNet confirming everything was OK and all parties knew.

> "Channel One resumes normal traffic. Normal traffic at 1326." I released the channel back to normal operations but felt confused since felony stops are usually longer. Without understanding, I made a mental note to circle back with D61 later.

Thankfully, I didn't have to wait long. D61 called into dispatch and advised the truck had been reported stolen a month ago and then recovered two days later. In a blunder, the vehicle was removed from the crime information system, but the plate was not. The registered owner had been driving the truck and was pulled out at gunpoint! *Whoops!* Clerical errors occasionally happen because of miscommunication, forgetfulness, or neglect. I made sure the plate was correctly removed from the system this time around.

Nearing the end of my shift, I returned from my break more haggard than usual. I settled back into my station to work the phones for the remainder of my shift. As fate would have it, my introduction to new technology was not yet complete. The agency I worked for always tried to stay on the cutting edge of 911 technology and had recently introduced software called RapidSOS. This platform displays the location of a 911 caller using data from phone manufacturers. To protect the privacy of many cell phone users, the platform will only display caller information for up to ten minutes after the 911 call has been disconnected. This technology provides impressively accurate location information, enhancing the capabilities of traditional 911 phone systems. Moreover, data from this platform confidently replaces a traditional phone ping, a very long and tedious process involving multiple phone calls to phone providers who make telecommunicators jump through a lot of hoops to get scraps of information. I was about to take my first RapidSOS test drive and never look back.

Looking at the clock and counting down the seconds until my shift was over and I could erase myself from this day and escape into my bed, I reached to answer the trilling emergency line. A panicked female voice spoke swiftly in my ear. I struggled to get information from her with my telecommunicator techniques. I first got her name and repeatedly used it to try and ground her, but nothing changed. Pulling out more tactics, I tried talking quieter and calmer. Nope. Then I raised my voice to talk over her. Strike two. She was crying and very upset, repeating to me how cold it was outside; indeed, it was twenty-three degrees. After these unsuccessful attempts, I worked to pinpoint her location with the usual resources, beginning with my standard resources, starting with my 911 phone technology. Staring at the familiar screen, I impatiently clicked the refresh button, willing the cell phone to resync with the tower and provide an updated location. Soon I was rewarded as the location updated from a preliminary phase one assessment to a more accurate phase two reading. Although phase two is better, these locations are still fallible and inaccurate. I entered cross streets, verified the location in CAD, and dropped a welfare check in the queue for dispatch. Even though I knew the location information could be inaccurate, I prioritized starting help while I worked to refine the exact location of my damsel in distress.

While quickly adding to my call for service, I continued to talk to the female and ascertain her exact location. She told me that a date kicked her out of the car. *Not such a nice date.* As she spoke to me about her horrible night through slurred words falling out of frigid lips, my deputy radioed that he was in the area and needed a description of her clothes.

"What are you wearing right now?" I asked, thinking about the Jake from State Farm commercial. She stuttered through a description of clothes that weren't appropriate for the cold temperatures, and I empathized with her.

"Have you been doing any drinking or drugs tonight?" I asked next to obtain pertinent officer safety information. The line disconnected. *Hmm.* I tried several times to call back. Each time she sent me straight to voicemail. Telecommunicator PSA: we do not intend to piss people off with these questions. The questions may sound scary, but the answers help first responders prepare their initial steps on a call. After ringing her a few more times, I knew she wasn't going to answer again. However, if I could get a better location, my deputy could still locate the needle in a haystack and get her the help she wanted before I made her mad. I knew she was somewhere within a two-block radius filled with businesses and residential condos. Within that two-block radius were three different police jurisdictions determined by the *lane of traffic*. As I contemplated the next steps, I remembered RapidSOS and quickly logged into this web-based application, popped her phone number in the search bar, and *boom*! Immediate location pin, sweet and simple. On the map, I could see her location updating as she moved. I amended the call for service with the location notes, and Channel One radioed the pertinent update to first responders.

My deputies in the area were able to redirect their search efforts and find an intoxicated female exactly where RapidSOS showed her stumbling around on the map. Considering the lack of information we started with, locating and assisting this caller represented a huge win for my team and me. According to the report, this female was highly intoxicated and could not offer the deputies a clear story or advise if a crime had occurred. Her recollections about her date were confusing, and her timeline of events changed a few times as she spoke. Based on this information, my deputy was unable to determine if a crime occurred, but he called for rescue to evaluate and transport the female to the hospital. At the end of the night, I was just glad we were able to find her! Without the technology pinpointing her precise location, units probably would not have been able to locate her. A drunk girl alone on the street in an unfamiliar place at night sounds like the premise of most *Law & Order: SVU* episodes. I told the room about this success, and everyone enthusiastically jumped on the RapidSOS train.

Shortly after this call, the graveyard shift walked in. My shoulders eased seeing them—I was about to go home. I watched as another telecommunicator signed in for the night. Remembering the issues we had earlier, I held my breath and said a prayer for her computer. She logged in, and her computer went through the ten-minute ordeal, then she launched her CAD and received an error message. *No, not this again!* She tried to log out and back in and try again. No luck. I advised her to shut down the computer and try again. She did that twice with no success. I tried with my sign-on, and still the same message displayed.

"You'll have to use a different computer tonight, Sasha. I'm sorry," I broke the news. *Darn you, IT!* I whisked myself to my office and furiously typed another email about the latest technology snafu. *Send!* My head sank into my hands, I took a deep breath, and I reminded myself: *there were wins today. Focus on the positive.* One final hour remaining in this excruciatingly long day, I returned to my chair and put on my headset.

Cardiopulmonary Resuscitation

Emma

Cardiopulmonary Resuscitation (CPR) is a lifesaving procedure performed when the heart stops beating. According to the American Heart Association, immediate CPR can double or triple the chances of survival after a cardiac arrest.[2] The immediate start of CPR is the act of getting "hands-on-chest." For telecommunicators trained in Emergency Medical Dispatching (EMD) protocols, CPR is one of the most impactful tools we have to save a life. A CPR call is also one of the most adrenaline-pumping, holy grail, chaotic calls possible. And like every other call, they are never the same twice.

EMD protocol is verified by doctors to ensure that instructions provided during emergencies are viable and accurate. Telecommunicators go through hours of training to ensure they give the instructions correctly, then during the call they must meet certain benchmarks to make sure everything is performed correctly. The gold standard to start "hands-on-chest," high-quality CPR is three minutes after the call begins. Experts have concluded this time frame gives the best chance of survival for a patient in cardiac arrest. Seems simple, right? In the same three minutes, a telecommunicator must also obtain and confirm a location, obtain and confirm a phone number, appropriately screen what is happening, get the patient in the right position and direct the (often) hysterical caller to listen to instructions and act with decisiveness. This list makes every CPR call a chance for a miracle.

To date, with almost ten years of experience, I have only had twenty CPR calls, and all of them varied with different levels of cooperation, aptitude, and end results. I have given instructions for CPR for overdoses, old people collapsing, and choking. In general, any time a patient is not conscious and not breathing, CPR should be used.

During my first CPR call, the adrenaline rush was real, and I can still feel it to this day: hands shaking uncontrollably, heart racing, and the closest thing to tunnel vision I have experienced.

"Help me! Help me, he's not breathing!" an RP screamed in my ear.

I took a deep breath, knowing what I needed to do. After verifying the location and paging out the fire department, I knew I needed to follow my EMD protocol. Luckily my female caller was very cooperative and did not fight instructions.

"Lay him flat on his back and remove any pillows from under his head," I said, reading my protocol card verbatim.

"OK, OK, hurry!" she said in a panic. I could hear rustling, so I knew she was following my instructions.

"I'm going to walk you through CPR instructions," I told her with my big girl voice. She informed me that someone was with her to help. This was very good news because two-rescuer CPR is always better for patient care. CPR is a workout, so when two people can share the burden and take turns, the thrusts are more impactful and better quality.

"Who is with you?" I asked.

"My brother is here. We were visiting with my dad and he just collapsed right in front of us!" she cried.

"Place one hand on his chest right between his nipples, then place the other hand on top of that hand," I told her. "You need to pump the chest hard and fast, at least twice per second and two inches deep." I continued reading off the card. This card doesn't advertise that the appropriate force will crack and break ribs. That always comes as a shock.

"We are going to do this 600 times or until help arrives. Count out loud, and I will count with you," I continued.

My partner dispatched the units while I continued to count with my RP. My adrenaline began to level out, my soccer captain persona kicked in, and I coached and encouraged her. We were one on the phone together. Counting in unison. Both with a common goal of saving a life.

"One and two and three and four!" I cajoled loud enough for others to hear on their phone calls. Only when our Animal Control officer later asked if the patient made it did I realize how loud I was. She heard me counting from the other side of the police department and wanted to check in. Sadly, despite best efforts all around and getting hands-on-chest in under three minutes, the patient didn't survive.

Throughout my career, each CPR call I've coached was unique, but one thing always is the same: the feeling of absolute pride and accomplishment when the fire department airs "ROSC" (Return of Spontaneous Circulation) or "patient is now conscious, alert, and breathing." Telecommunicators don't expect recognition for saving a life, but the rush that it brings is unmatched. My first attempt at CPR with a caller had a sad ending, but I am extremely proud of three ROSCs, and one life saved.

Lea

I am amazed at what people think they can get away with when the sun is up. Half my career I worked during the day and half I worked at night. After my years in 911 I can confidently conclude that the cover of darkness is the preferred time for crime! Fewer people in the stillness of night means less traffic and fewer eyes observing wayward actions. Regardless of the advantages of nighttime crime, some criminals will boldly act in broad daylight.

On one such day, our PSAP navigated a legitimate crime spree. A crime spree, for those who don't religiously watch *Dateline* every Friday night, is a series of crimes committed in quick succession. In this case, it was not only street scandalous but also created serious waves in the communication center.

It was a Wednesday in November, and the air was crisp. A perfect fall day. Snow had covered the ground two days prior, but on this day, beautiful weather prevailed, leaving only mounds of crunchy, shoveled snow to the left and right of the sidewalks. The afterthought snow. Nothing atypical happened that morning. I left for my break at eleven o'clock and ate a sandwich in the breakroom. I shut my eyes for a moment, but IT was in the next room loudly messing with the radio control unit and interrupting my sacred quiet time. I was mildly annoyed. Realizing no time at work is ever peaceful, I washed my dirty dishes and returned to the dispatching floor. As I walked back to the west side workstations where on-duty personnel typically sat, I noticed that the phones weren't ringing, the radio traffic was minimal, and everyone was relaxed. Talia colored. Allison browsed the internet.

"Hey Allison, your lunch is calling!" I said with a smile while I put my headset on. Just then a 911 call shattered the peaceful silence. I answered. The male caller spoke quickly and urgently with that special tone of voice that makes any 911 telecommunicator sit up straight in the chair. I knew the situation was dire. He had my full, undivided attention. This was not an animal complaint, cold shoplifting, or a noise violation. This was an emergency.

The RP swiftly gave me the location: a local recreation center. Knowing the address by heart, I quickly added it to my location field and listened in for more details.

"I heard gunshots. Sounds like they came from behind the building!" he spurted. I typed a simple narrative into my call: "shots fired." The call, now in the CAD queue, was accessible for Talia to dispatch.

"Go to the rec center!" I hollered across the room to her, covering my microphone so as not to interrupt the stream of information my RP was spouting. This was a tip my trainer taught me. If you have a hot (i.e., emergent) call, alert the room. Although the primary channel telecommunicators are trained to continuously check the call queue, even sitting feet away they may miss a critical call being dropped in. It's an old-school method of teamwork. I immediately heard my dispatch partner sound the high-pitched alert tone. *Hallelujah, units are started!* Because of the proximity of the police department to the recreation center, I knew first responders would be there in a matter of seconds. I focused my attention on getting as much detail as I could from the caller.

Where are the shots coming from? Do you see the shooters? Is anyone injured? Unfortunately, this RP didn't have a ton of information. He heard the shots and people screaming about a gunman. He thought they were in the rear of the building. He was a manager at the center so, despite his lack of information, I told him to follow his protocol and lock down the building for safety. He complied, and I confirmed all his contact information for the future. I knew he would be a key player moving forward.

When working an intense situation like this, it's not long before the PSAP is inundated with calls from the many people who heard or saw the commotion. Soon our phone lines were full, and we couldn't keep up with the call volume. Lines were rolling over to our backup center, but we triaged the incoming flux as best we could, placing many callers on hold. I hung up with my first RP and quickly moved to the next call, a female neighbor who saw activity at the bus depot behind the rec center. She witnessed two subjects crash a car and start shooting. She mentioned the same males were now hidden in the outbuildings. *Thank you, Jesus!* This RP had good information. I added descriptions and this narrative to the call notes for immediate need and context—two males crashed a car, started shooting, and were now hiding. No time to think, I obtained this RP's information and hopped on the next call. And the next. And the next.

In the middle of this storm, I saw a ray of bright light when Joy, a former telecommunicator who'd recently switched departments, entered the PSAP. She ran into the room with her headset around her neck, ready to take calls. *Wow.* The very definition of dedication and teamwork—once a telecommunicator, always a telecommunicator. My next call was from Lakewood PD, who advised they had been trying to contact us on MetroNet. A carjacking had occurred in their city, and the suspects were headed in our direction. *Oh great.* Suddenly, this crashed car narrative made more sense. I got her information and shared that we were already working the tail end of her story. I quickly brought this telecommunicator up to speed about the events in my city and asked that she start resources my way for joint investigations and mutual aid.

As we continued answering calls and collecting information, time sped up and slowed down all at once. We maintained sanity in the time warp by focusing on the next task. An hour later, as time and the call volume slowed enough to hear our thoughts again, the team started to dissect the incident in a mini-debriefing session. Everyone turned their chairs to face each other and informally discussed our calls and roles. Shock reverberated throughout the room. The day had gone from zero to 100 in ten seconds. Everyone was so happy that Joy came to help, and they offered her an abundance of thanks and praise. Another coworker expressed sympathy recalling her conversation with a daughter whose mom was injured from the gunfire. Although the mother's injuries didn't seem life-threatening, she was still worried. A somber silence fell heavy on the room.

"Did anyone read my narrative from Lakewood?" I piped up with a tone of consternation. I assessed all their faces as they nodded in agreement.

"It would have been nice to know that this was coming our way!" my supervisor said, echoing the sentiments of many. We all shrugged and continued working, content that there were no casualties, and that police response time was swift.

Everyone moved on to the next emergencies, radio transmissions, and requests as if we hadn't just worked an active shooter incident. Sometime later, we finally had the whole story, thanks to an officer calling and filling in the details. Three males, wearing *Scream* masks, robbed a bank in Lakewood around ten thirty in the morning. They got in their getaway car but made a last-minute decision to switch vehicles to better evade detection. Continuing to drive, they canvassed for a car to steal. Unfortunately, they found a lovely old man who was warming up his car in the alleyway before a doctor's appointment. The suspects assaulted and shot him, leaving him crumpled in a dirty snowbank. Despite his condition, he called 911, alerting police to the bank robbers' location. Officers were in the area, quickly located the vehicle, and began pursuing the suspects. As the suspects drove, more agencies joined the pursuit that spanned four Denver area police jurisdictions. The suspects continued tearing southbound through the metro area. At this point, Lakewood PD tried to warn us via MetroNet. Our center did not answer. Lakewood PD, inundated with calls, did not attempt to reach us by phone.

Just after noon, the calamity screeched to a halt when the bandits crashed their car in the parking lot of the rec center. They spied a mother and daughter getting into their vehicle after a Zumba class. In an evil bid for another getaway car, a suspect shot the woman with the keys, leaving her in a parking lot snow pile. In what could be considered a moment of divine providence, the vehicle did not start, so the suspects ran for cover in the bus depot behind the rec center. Officers arrived quickly and fanned out looking for multiple suspects. They located one suspect assaulting a bus driver. Meanwhile, the other two suspects evaded custody despite an extensive search that shut down multiple city blocks for several hours.

The entire crime spree came into sharp focus, and the FBI helped local PD deduce that our suspects were indeed the "*Scream*-Masked Bandits" who had been infamously robbing banks in the Denver area. They were distinguishable by the masks and a violent takeover technique. Not good people.

Six days after this incident, a team of investigators, in conjunction with the FBI, located the second suspect. The third was still at-large and made an appearance on the FBI's most wanted list for about three months before his capture. Eighteen months later, these three individuals were sentenced to a combined 3,459 years in prison. Both shooting victims healed with minimal residual damage from their wounds—an absolute miracle, especially considering the elderly man in the alley was shot six times. Six.

I remember this day, not only because most telecommunicators will never answer this type of call in their careers, but also because this was my first experience with internal affairs.

Internal affairs, or IA, is the unit within every police agency that polices the cops. IA investigates misconduct, poor job performance, bribes, sexual harassment, and other related topics. The chief of police for the city opened a complaint citing negligence of duties within our communication center after he discovered Lakewood tried to warn us several times via MetroNet about the impending pursuit. *Yes, we can agree sir, it would have been nice to know ahead of time!*

This complaint introduced me to the world of internal affairs investigations. Radio traffic recordings were pulled, and we were all interviewed about the events of the day. MetroNet recordings proved that Lakewood had tried to reach us several times. However, MetroNet is an ancillary radio channel secondary to Channels One and Two; it is not monitored 24/7. Good telecommunicators can monitor multiple channels at once. Great telecommunicator teams often have members who turn up primary and peripheral radio channels so that no call for aid is overlooked. The team working that day had over forty years of dispatching experience. Stellar, senior people. But no one in that room heard MetroNet. Not one.

In my IA interview, I recalled that I returned from lunch at the top of the hour (during Lakewood's final attempt to reach us) and walked into a very quiet dispatch center. I also mentioned that several IT employees were working on the radio console in the back of the center. I told the investigator that I truly believed this is why we didn't hear the MetroNet traffic. There had to be some interference. Two of our PSAP's most experienced telecommunicators, including a supervisor and a lead trainer, typically monitor the MetroNet with high attention. It raises questions why these transmissions were missed. Additionally, I wondered about the delay in communication from Lakewood. Standard procedure usually requires a phone call if radio contact isn't successful. However, the first call from Lakewood was made two minutes *after* the reported shots at the rec center, despite them having a fourteen-minute advance notice of the situation.

A radio console interruption caused by IT that day was never proven, but it did cause reasonable doubt. In the end, our entire team got slapped on the wrist with official letters in our files. More significantly, after the investigation our bureau chief mandated the volume of MetroNet be locked on every console to a minimum of three (out of five). That day started a long history of complaints amongst call-takers and radio telecommunicators because MetroNet blared over RPs and radio traffic, making it difficult to think straight.

In the end, I know my team did a great job with this incident, and we helped justice to be served for the innocent victims and the criminals who tried to take their lives. A slap on the wrist and a letter in my file could never take that away.

Emma

I have a love-hate relationship with the Safe2Tell program. It was established in Colorado as a way for kids in school to anonymously report anything they are facing. Suicide. Drinking. Drugs. Wild parties. Cheating. Sexual abuse. Depression. You name it, kids and adults can report it using the Safe2Tell program. However, mix anonymity with school-aged kids, and you often get a tattletale network! Most of the "tips" received resemble the Johnny-was-vaping-in-the-bathroom or my-teacher-was-mean-to-me-today-because-she-made-me-do-homework kind of information. Every tip is filtered through a large list of personnel, including night shift telecommunicators, SROs, school principals, and guidance counselors. You can imagine the colossal waste of time created by non-legitimate tips. But once in a blue moon, a Safe2Tell is right on point.

Bing! My computer dings and a "Make sure you check the Safe2Tell folder" automated message pops up.

"I got it!" I hollered to my team, knowing everyone hated them. I knew doing it myself would squash any complaining and leave one less menial task to fall through the cracks during the shift change.

These reports are intentionally very generic.

Date:
Time:
Name of school:
Name of the involved:
Grade/age:
What is happening:
Any additional information:

Normally these forms come back with one line of description per prompt (if we are lucky) and lots of misspelled words. Yes, they are only adolescents, but some correct grammar would be nice. In this specific situation, the anonymous informant provided a friend's name and age, and that she had posted on her social media that she had cut her wrists and wanted to die.

OH! I sat up straight. This might be a serious Safe2Tell. Armed with similar resources that police officers have, I started digging. Telecommunicators are given high clearances to ensure proper investigation into situations like these and to make sure units have complete information before and during calls they respond to. Announcing to the police "a sixteen-year-old girl cut her wrists somewhere in the city" would serve no one. I couldn't send up a signal for Batman to find her. Telecommunicators are the Batmans. *We* find her.

I searched every resource I could imagine. First, I checked the priors on her name. Have we ever had contact with her? That would easily beef up my call. No luck there. Next, I searched my database for a possible driver's license. Unfortunately, she had a fairly common name, and she shared it with several others in the city. But I was able to glean a few last names and dates of birth that could match, then I looked at my map and deduced the most likely candidates based on the school she attended. The search significantly narrowed. I was able to cross-verify the known school, the name, and the age of the girl to determine the correct location.

I updated my call notes and gave my officer a heads-up, pridefully confident in all of my information. During his response I noticed he had called the home phone number I provided and had advised the parents of the situation. Coupled with his emergent response, this helped the situation reach the best possible outcome. He met with the parents immediately after arriving on scene, and they all went up together to check on the subject. She was at home, bleeding out from very deep cuts on her wrist. My unit called for an ambulance, and she was transported to the hospital where she got proper medical treatment and made a full recovery.

In the end, the officer gave me kudos for my stellar work. If not for my research and timely attention to detail, she very easily could have died. Any more time wasted rolling eyes about Safe2Tell reports or inexperience in dispatch detective skills and help might not have arrived in time. Being behind the computer doesn't always make a difference, but in this case, it very clearly did. After that day, I thought differently about Safe2Tells. That anonymous friend helped save a life.

Lea

No one is perfect. But when someone's life hangs in the balance, mistakes carry more serious consequences, and every telecommunicator constantly feels that burden. Owning shortcomings is the most important aspect of any job; any problem becomes ten times worse if you deflect, lie, or cover it up. Luckily, in my career I never screwed up badly enough to get anyone hurt or injured—unlike a few horror stories that everyone in emergency services knows about. A telecommunicator in Florida was fired for failing to air an updated sighting of a suspicious vehicle involved in the kidnapping of a neighboring detective's young daughter. The same vehicle was found later with her lifeless body inside the trunk. Similarly in Texas, a telecommunicator was sued because she hung up on an escalated caller reporting a medical emergency and didn't send help. In another instance, tragedy struck Ohio residents after a teenage boy was crushed by the seat inside his minivan. He had called 911, and the dispatch center displayed negligence for improperly triaging his calls.

Stakes are high. Margin for error is nil. There are no do-overs.

While I do carry some shame about the mistakes I made during my career, I owned every one of them. Falling on my own sword and displaying integrity was a lesson I learned early and practiced often.

My most memorable lesson happened when a coworker, known for *frequent* trips to the break room, asked me to listen to Channel One because he forgot something. Again. *Didn't he just return from break?*

"Sure," I said, trying to hide my irritation as I clicked into Channel One.

It was a long day training a recruit on phones, and I was ready to go home. We had finished taking calls for the day and situated ourselves in the back pod, away from everyone else, studying the training manual together for her upcoming phone phase test. With thirty minutes remaining, I watched the clock tick. Giving myself a quick attitude adjustment, I seized the learning opportunity for my phone trainee.

"Hey Sasha, click into Channel One with me. I am listening for Larry." I watched her excitedly shove her books aside and click into the radio to listen in. Noticing she clicked into the right radio on the first try, I felt a promising tinge of joy. I was still relatively new to dispatching myself; in hindsight I should have just shut up and focused on listening to Channel One instead of talking about Channel One.

I was rambling about something when a high priority call dropped into the queue. Sitting in the back pod, I didn't hear my teammate taking the 911 call, and no one thought to alert me. Soon enough deputies self-dispatched themselves to the call using CAD on their car computers. I didn't even see the call for service in queue before deputies self-assigned. Didn't even read it. Didn't even air it. I was too busy chatting about the importance of Channel One; meanwhile several deputies were now responding to a domestic disturbance call involving a knife! My stomach still turns at the thought.

Larry returned from the bathroom, or wherever he was, and said, "Thanks for listening. I got it."

"Cool. Nothing happened," I reported.

"Edward 51, I'm on scene at Parker. Can I have the air until cover arrives?" I heard this transmission as I clicked out of the channel. My eyes widened and my stomach dropped.

"Holy shit!" Larry yelled.

My heart sank. I pulled up the call, and my cheeks flushed with horror. It was a Priority One call. Per policy, all calls of that nature, especially with weapons involved, had to be verbally aired and toned for situational awareness. Because of my negligence, nothing was aired and I put several first responders' lives at risk. What is more, I hadn't correctly briefed Larry when he came back. I told him nothing was going on, which was very far from the truth. I didn't do my job.

As I was stewing in shame, my supervisor hollered for me to sign off. This event put a bright red exclamation point at the end of my shift. With a pit in my stomach and tears running hot down my face, I signed off and then approached my supervisor to rat myself out. I told her I wasn't paying attention and that the call should have been toned. I said it wasn't Larry's fault. She thanked me for being honest. I told her I felt horrible and asked if I should go talk to the lieutenant.

"That's a good idea. But don't cry all over him," she advised, noting my current condition.

I walked downstairs to the patrol offices and bolstered up the courage to enter my lieutenant's office and tell him what happened. I wiped my face and rounded the corner. I found him sitting in his office, and I knocked to announce my presence.

"Lieutenant Wakeman? May I speak with you?" I asked sheepishly.

"Sure!" he said cheerfully. He was always a jovial man. He didn't know me, and I was certain after he found out what I did, the happy tone would wear off.

"Uh, my name is Lea Harms. I was the Channel One telecommunicator during that Parker call a few minutes ago." I looked up, and his eyes were dead set on mine. "I came down here to apologize for not doing my job. I realized that call needed to be aired. I am sorry."

"Aired, but most importantly toned, too," he said matter-of-factly. "It was a priority call with weapons involved. Toning this type of call sets the precedent and lets everyone on the radio know."

"I know, sir. I am sorry. I have a phone trainee, and I was clicked in with her and talking to her about Channel One functions, and I didn't even see the call go in. It is not an excuse—I should have been focused only on Channel One, not on telling her about Channel One. I am sorry, and it won't happen again," I said steadfastly.

"Thanks for saying that. No one got hurt. My job at the end of the day is to make sure all these folks go home to their families. It's your job, too," he reminded me with kindness, but the message was poignant.

"Of course, sir. It was nice to meet you. I'll talk to you later." I excused myself, shaking his hand before I left.

I held my breath until I reached a safe distance away, then exhaled. *Whew.* To this day, that is still one of the most humbling and rewarding things I have ever done. This moment taught me a lot about who I am and my capacity to take ownership of my wrongdoings. I also realized how much grace the friendly lieutenant offered me, and how I can do the same for others. Years later as a shift supervisor, I brought one of my staff members into my office to address a clerical error she made, and I remembered this conversation. Her error, made the night before, caused an innocent motorist to be suspected of driving a stolen vehicle and pulled out of his truck at gunpoint. She sat down, knowing what was coming, and her face immediately turned beet red. Seeing so much of myself in her felt like looking in a mirror at that moment. When I spoke to her about her mix-up (juxtaposing two numbers!), I spoke with respect and dignity. Knowing her own shame would do the impactful work for me, I focused on encouraging her to continue being diligent.

Just as I grew to be one of the best Channel One telecommunicators in my PSAP, I knew she too would grow to be a great asset. Grace inspires greatness.

Lea

The *Walking Dead*, as you probably know, is a zombie show that takes place in the postapocalyptic USA where droves of humans have become biting, entrail-eating zombies. Survivors fight tooth and nail through each episode to endure the new world order. The artistic directors and make-up folks on the show created rotted flesh and glazed eyes with frightening accuracy. These are scary zombies. I couldn't help but think about these creatures one warm May evening as I encountered a real-life zombie.

This night, my coworkers and I sat talking while playing a game of Phase 10. A 911 call interrupted our festivities, and I rolled across the room to my console to stifle the high-pitched tone. Picking up the phone I instantly heard a female's deafening screams. My adrenaline started pumping, and immediately I switched gears from collecting sets and runs mode to telecommunicator mode. Slow, deep breaths provided me laser focus, and I was ready to go.

Keeping a calm voice can instinctively force the caller to lower their volume to hear what you are saying, but after attempting that tactic, I realized that wasn't going to work with this caller. She needed someone to take control and gain her attention.

"HE SHOT HIMSELF!" she screamed repeatedly. I yelled over her to get her attention, and she complied. I needed the address, which she provided. I recognized the address as an apartment complex nearby.

"OK, so he shot himself," I stated. Some callers get irritated when we repeat information they just relayed, but this tactic serves two purposes. First, it makes the caller pause to hear their information repeated back to them. In high-stress situations, this can give a telecommunicator ample time to write crucial notes or gain ground on an emotional caller. Second, it serves as a verbal cue to my radio person across the room to prepare for a call in the queue that needs immediate attention. I saw both my coworkers, picking up on my cues, leave the game table for their workstations. My intensity with this caller was palpable.

I dropped the call in the queue as a "completed suicide," a common notation for someone who has shot themself. As I continued to talk to my RP, I saw unit assignments had been made and deputies were en route after only forty-five seconds of call triage. Returning my focus to the caller, I asked questions to better understand his injuries.

"Is he conscious and breathing?" I asked.

"Yes," she stated. *WHAT?* My jaw dropped and my fingers paused before recording that narrative.

"Wait. What? He is alive?" Jordan exclaimed from her side of the room, matching my surprise.

I turned and nodded, my eyes bugging out, and gave nonverbal confirmation. She aired the information to responding officers, her tone oozing disbelief. I decided to transfer the call to rescue so they could provide lifesaving instructions like CPR and wound management. Before I did this, I needed to know one more thing for my officers' safety.

"Where is the gun?" I asked.

"I threw it on the bed out of reach," she managed to tell me through sobs. With that, I transferred the call to rescue, and they controlled the remainder of the call. I muted myself so I could continue to listen and provide necessary updates to police responders. I discovered the patient was a thirty-five-year-old male who shot himself in the head with a 9 mm handgun in his apartment. Normally, when people shoot themselves in the head, they don't survive. One study in *JAMA Ophthalmology* projects that surviving a self-initiated gunshot wound to the head represents 1 percent of all failed suicide attempts.[3] *One percent.*

Over rescue's efforts, I could hear a male's voice moaning and talking. Meanwhile the RP was describing a horrible picture of the patient crawling on the floor, like he was looking for something. Envisioning this, I could only imagine the scene my deputies were about to find. I checked their AVL (Automatic Vehicle Locators) to see where they were. Their lights and sirens response finally brought them close as the rescue telecommunicator instructed the caller to get clean towels and put them firmly on the wound.

The RP was frazzled—her husband was agitated, and she couldn't calm him enough to get close and apply firm towel pressure as instructed. I cringed thinking about his excruciating pain and her absolute horror. In the middle of all of this, I could hear loud moaning and shouting.

"Get away from me! Leave me alone!" With no slurring or slowness to his words, the victim was clearly refusing help.

"He is crawling away from me. He won't let me touch him," the RP whimpered.

Hearing this, the rescue telecommunicator switched tactics, advising her to stay a safe distance away from him. Fearing for her safety in a potentially escalated situation, he told the wife to just wait. Akin to a wounded animal lashing out if you come too close, a victim might not trust your help. In this situation, even his wife was an enemy.

The fire department telecommunicator asked what happened that led to this point. The sobbing RP told a familiar story. The couple had some friends over that evening. All ex-military folks. Everyone was drinking. Her husband got drunk, and the laughter turned to terror. The two husbands started to wrestle and act like men do. Bravado. The question was posed—who would win a match? The caller advised that she openly stated her husband would lose. After the friends left and the party was over, an argument ensued. Her husband's ego was severely bruised, and he was very drunk—a deadly combination. As the fight escalated, he grabbed his gun and exclaimed something about self-worth before putting the gun to his temple and pulling the trigger.

Pop.

Down he went. Here we were.

My deputies arrived two minutes after the initial 911 call. Two minutes felt like an eternity. The RP saw the deputies and hung up. I took a deep breath, and the room behind me was silent. Now we waited. We resumed our game of Phase 10, and between rounds, updates came slowly. Five minutes after they arrived at the scene, deputies advised they were riding with the patient in the ambulance to the nearest local hospital. Then nothing. Another long wait. More Phase 10. An hour later, a deputy dispo'd (provided a disposition of) the call with a case report.

Normally the story would end here. In dispatch we don't always get the full story. In this case, I persistently pursued more information because of my level of involvement and my personal relationship with the responding deputy. I asked for a full report, and my deputy filled in the blanks. The story he told and the picture he showed me still haunt me.

He recounted running up the stairs and opening the door. He cautiously entered and found the patient crawling around the floor, as described, in a mess of blood and brain matter. The deputy immediately moved to secure the weapon, the priority of any law enforcement officer. As he was assessing the situation and establishing rapport with the patient, rescue units arrived. The four-man team quickly and efficiently brought the patient from a crawling stance to a prone position on the floor and loaded him on the stretcher. My friend rode with the crew to the hospital and asked the patient questions about what had happened, what his name was, how old he was, how much he drank. He answered all the questions perfectly. No slurring. Clear. In the middle of these questions, EMTs peppered him with basic questions: what was two plus two, what was five times zero. The patient provided every answer confidently without error. The ambulance pulled into the bay, the patient was rushed into the ER, and a team of doctors began asking him the same kinds of questions. According to my deputy, he continued to respond, but now his answers made no sense. Utter nonsense spilled out of his mouth, in stark contrast to the ambulance ride just five minutes before.

About a half hour later, the doctor came out to meet with the family with bad news. The patient would lose brain function in a day or so; he did not have long to live. The bullet had entered his head in the eye socket, ricocheted off his skull, and exited the side of his face near the ear. He inadvertently lobotomized himself.

His wife was devastated. She had two small children. All this horror because of a drunken bruised ego.

I asked to see a picture of the victim, and it wasn't what I was expecting. I feared the worst—a large, gaping hole in his head. Instead, he looked like a comic book villain. One side of his face was smooth and normal. The other side was puffy and disfigured, like he lost a fight with the world's largest bee. His eye was swollen shut where the bullet had entered, and the exit wound was clearly visible on the same side of his head. When I close my eyes, I still see his face, less like Rick Grimes and more like Solomon Grundy, haunting my dreams.

How the Grinch Saved Christmas

Lea

My husband, Spencer, loves this next story. First, it doesn't involve any blood or death. Second, and most importantly, because it involves Christmas. He is a Christmas fanatic. One of my favorite things about him is that he has no shame messaging me in the middle of August when it is 8,000 degrees outside with a Spotify screenshot of the Christmas classics he is listening to. He is a lost cause.

Holidays in the center were generally...strange. Grinchy even? Mostly because we were all working with a touch of homesickness. While our families gathered to eat, drink, and be merry, we slaved away trying to siphon the holiday spirit with movie marathons while potluck Crock-Pots burned their contents. Emergency service shift work doesn't stop for family holiday gatherings.

I was training Allison, the center's newest recruit, on phones one Christmas Eve, sitting together with her at the same console. This was always an awkwardly intimate experience. In order to provide guidance, we had to throw out all rules of proximity and personal space. Bad breath, gas, body odor—so many uncomfortable possibilities!

That night I sat perched over my trainee's shoulder to watch her take calls. I liked her a lot. She was smart and a quick study; I could tell she would do well. A 911 call rang in, and she dutifully reached to answer. As she connected to the line, a little voice on the other end greeted us. *Again.* This kiddo had called nonstop for the last hour on a disconnected cell phone. (FYI: disconnected cell phones can still call 911. Do not give them to your children for entertainment. Please.)

The youngster babbled about nothing important, and we were unable to obtain his location. Every disconnected cell phone rings in with a 911 area code, which is not compatible with reverse searches, provider pings, or RapidSOS. As he babbled, I wanted nothing more than to find this kid and enroll him and his parents in the "dispatch scared-straight program."

This tot was effectively taking away time from other 911 callers with actual emergencies.

"Can I speak to your mommy or daddy?" Allison politely asked.

"Mommy not home," the tot said plainly. All lies, I was sure. *Click.* The phone hung up for the twenty-eighth time.

After this call, I discussed with Allison how she handled the call and how our efforts needed to be more persuasive the next time.

"Do you have kids?" I asked her.

"Yes, a two-year-old," she said, and she began telling me about her daughter.

"Sometimes a 'mom voice' will get a kid's attention better than sweetly asking for Mommy or Daddy," I stated matter-of-factly. She nodded and agreed, on board with our mission.

A short time later, she answered another 911, and there was that little voice again. This time Allison used her best stern "mom voice" to get the kid's attention. He didn't respond well and disconnected promptly.

"That was better! I think we may have scared him a little!" I exclaimed. That praise was short-lived as another 911 call came in with the same little voice. *Seriously?* This kid was driving everyone in the center nuts. I wasn't leaving this call to my trainee. I was fed up and tired of the games.

I motioned that I wanted to take over the call and uncovered my mic.

"Hey!" I said, with a friendly and excited tone. "You know who I work for? I work for Santa! If you don't give this phone to Momma or Daddy right now, then Santa won't bring you any presents tonight," I said, going straight for the jugular. *Playtime is over, kid.*

Immediately, I heard scrambling around and a lot of movement. The phone was moving quite a bit.

"Hola?" an adult female voice asked with confusion.

"Hi there. This is 911. Your son keeps dialing us?" I stated, praying that she spoke English.

"Ooooooohhhhh my gosh. I am so sorry!" she gasped, very alert now. *Boom.* I knew we landed and could officially kiss these irritating calls goodbye!

"Your kiddo has been playing with a disconnected cell phone," I told her. "I think he has called twenty times tonight. These phones aren't toys because they can still dial 911. We would appreciate it if you would take it away," I stated, repeating my best lines from the 911 education programs.

"I am so sorry. I understand. Thank you," she uttered.

"No problem. Merry Christmas!" I offered with a smile, hoping to lighten the mood.

"You too," she said with a hint of laughter in her voice.

And there you have it
Another notch in my kit.
A child's innocence you never forget.
Welcome, Christmas, from here to Tibet.
Maybe Christmas, she thought, will do the trick
Maybe Christmas, perhaps, will banish the prick.
And what happened then? Well, in Dispatchville they say
That the telecommunicator's small heart grew three sizes that day!
And then the true meaning of Christmas came through,
Trainees and parents both learned anew.
Welcome, Christmas, while we stand
Heart to heart and headset in hand.

Lea

"**S**o, on a scale from one to ten, what was that scene like?" I asked a seasoned sergeant on a recorded line to rank the grueling suicide he just responded to.

"Definitely one of the worst in my nineteen years. A solid nine," he said with a sigh. (Skip this chapter if you need to.)

"Yikes," I said, knowing his aptitude for these kinds of calls.

At five thirty in the morning, we were winding down a busy graveyard shift. I was on the main radio, lazily screening calls. All caught up, I started watching the clock tick, praying my eyes wouldn't close for too long and my head wouldn't bob—that level of exhaustion when you are so tired, your eyes shut for just a moment then your whole head sinks and startles you awake? *Hang in there, Lea. Just ninety more minutes.*

A 911 rang, and my coworker, Anita, answered. Immediately, her tone of voice and language told me it was a "real" call. As a very experienced dispatcher, nothing rocked her boat. She also was not known for her empathy with callers. But she began to use phrases like, "We know you didn't mean to," and "You did a good job," and "It is going to be OK. We are getting help out to you." Something was definitely up.

I peered across the room, curious about her delay in dropping a call into the queue. She looked fervently at her map and then back to her CAD; obviously the caller didn't know his location, so Anita used many resources to get a call for service entered for dispatch. She asked about mile markers and used clarifying statements like *eastbound or westbound*, which told me this call would be in Precinct 8, a vast, remote area with a large interstate running through it. Usually only one deputy services this part of the county. Coincidentally, at the time of the call, there were two cars on duty, a graveyard car left over from the night before and the early day shift car. I strategized the call assignment to the early day shift car so that the graveyard car didn't get stuck staying late and writing the report. Having a game plan when the call dropped into the queue I instantly aired,

"David 81 break and copy a suicide attempt. . ."

"Go ahead," he stated groggily. *Good morning sunshine! Time to work.*

Before I could enter the command to assign the dayshift car, the graveyard deputy picked up the call, making him the primary unit. *Ugh!* I tried to save him some work, but some folks just can't help themselves.

I continued airing the information. It boiled down to these basics: Anita talked on an emergency line to a truck driver who had been heading eastbound on the interstate near the county line. A woman with long hair stepped out from the dark, directly into his tractor trailer headlights. Hands up and eyes shut. There was no avoiding her. Impact was inevitable. The truck driver kept repeating, "she flew." After he pulled over and parked the eighteen-wheeler, he estimated she was a quarter of a mile behind him. The driver was in complete shock. He advised he had been driving trucks for eighteen years and this had never happened. Unfortunately, in a split second he became part of a really crappy trucker club. My heart went out to him. Same for Anita, who I know rarely displayed empathy for any caller after her two decades in the hot seat. Anita attempted to comfort and calm him. His panic was tangible.

Meanwhile, I went into hyperdrive to get multiple units dispatched to the call, air updates, call rescue, talk on MetroNet and ask for mutual aid to shut down the highway, and put calls on hold because apparently at that moment the phones needed to get busy. *Thank you, universe!* A deputy requested our victim advocate, and I made that notification. Dispatch was currently a two-man circus, and I was the ringleader.

"Is rescue going?" my lieutenant asked. I rolled my eyes and laughed while my hands flew across the keyboard.

"Yes sir, I started them three minutes ago." I tried to say sugary sweet to hide my irritation at his question. This wasn't my first day. Of course, I had started rescue for the woman that got hit by the tractor trailer.

"Paul 60 traffic," a traffic car called.

"Paul 60 go ahead," I said through gritted teeth.

Really? We were working a major call, and this fool had the nerve to initiate a traffic stop in the middle of a crap storm. What kind of egregious traffic violation would possess this deputy to grace my radio at this very moment? I made a mental note to berate him later then returned to doing the zillion other things I had to do.

Finally, a deputy arrived on scene. His response took just over four minutes, but in those four minutes, time froze. Anita confirmed the truck driver could see the deputy and indicated that his vehicle was in the right area to find the victim. I relayed this information to my unit, who was hindered by the dark of the early morning.

"Uh, this is an obvious DOA, so we can cancel rescue," he shakily stated a minute after arriving on scene. My heart sank with that knowledge, but then I smirked. The deputy, clearly new, forgot that rescue still had to respond to assess if life-saving efforts were needed and to perform a pronouncement.

"Frank 10, copy? Should rescue be canceled?" I asked, knowing the answer but needing his superiors to tell the newbie how to do his job.

"Keep them coming for pronouncement," F10 surmised. I nodded a note of thanks.

"Hey, Lea. This caller isn't doing well. Can 81 go talk to him?" Anita asked me from across the room.

"Frank 81, we are still landline with the caller, and he isn't doing well," I nudged on the radio.

"OK," he replied, his voice shaking. "I will make my way over."

I could tell from his tone that the scene was ghastly. I knew he had less than a year on the road, but whatever he was seeing was rocking him to the core. Behind me, I could hear my partner continue advising the trucker to take deep breaths, gently encouraging him. Her work with this RP was exceptional. She soon disconnected and began phoning the Department of Transportation, on-call investigators, evidence folks, and finally the coroner. Day shift telecommunicators started to arrive, bringing sweet, sweet relief. I informed the new supervisor of the horrible call we were ending, and she rallied her team to hurry through the briefing and join us on the floor.

Between our phone calls, we discussed our twisted telecommunicator thoughts. *What drove her to a horrible death? What does something like this even look like?*

"Lea, I am in." My radio relief interrupted these dark questions and assumed Channel One duties.

"OK, what you see is what you get. They are going to be shutting down the highway soon." I rattled off the details of the call. I signed out and dismissed my shift mates. We collected our belongings and started the trek to our cars.

"You OK?" I asked Anita halfway down the stairs.

"Yeah. I feel bad for him," she remarked.

"Me too. You did a really good job," I replied with a small smile. And thus ended another night in dispatch.

The next day my day shift friend messaged me and told me what she ascertained about the call. First, the suicidal subject was a he, not a she. The truck driver only thought he was a woman because of his long hair. Apparently, the deputies on scene also couldn't immediately determine because of the condition of the body. They too saw the long hair, and they also noted the fingernails appeared red, as if painted. However, the coroner quickly determined the subject was in fact a male after an anatomy check. The nails only appeared painted red because of the sheer force of being hit by a semitruck traveling at 80 mph. With this trauma, all the blood rushed to the extremities of the body, making the fingernails appear bright red. *Today I learned. . .* Additionally, sheriff's office deputies had contacted the man who was hit three hours prior at a trailer park near the highway. The subject was being "non-compliant" and acting "erratically," so his family called 911 requesting help. The same deputy who arrived on scene of the suicide was the same one who responded earlier and spoke with him and his family—a truly tragic ending to the night. When I clocked in the next night, I intentionally emailed my deputies and checked on them. They both replied that they were shocked but managing.

At the end of the day, five responders were polled and asked to rate the scene.

Responding deputy, three years with agency: 10/10
Victim Advocate, five years with this agency: 13/10
Coroner, two years with the agency: 8/10
Firefighter, 8 years with the department: 9/10

Anita and I never weighed in. But just because we didn't see it doesn't mean we didn't live it too.

Emma

One thing I have learned above all else is to expect the unexpected. Whether dealing with life-threatening emergencies, funny situations, death, nauseating detail, or moments of what-the-heck-just-happened—nothing is predictable.

A typical fraud report began innocently enough. An older lady got scammed out of some money because some jerk pretended to be her grandson needing to be bailed out of jail. This is a pretty common phone con targeting the elderly. Because they are less tech-savvy, live alone, and are easy to manipulate, they are one of our country's most vulnerable populations.

My older informant ranted about how she knew it was a scam, and that she does all these things to throw off the scammers, such as pushing random buttons on the phone, and then hangs up on them. She was quite the smart cookie, even though none of those things worked in this scenario, or any scenario.

"Thank you for your help, honey. Can I sing you a song?" my RP stated out of the blue.

"Sure!" I replied. *Why did I say that?* I am more of the get-the-facts-and-get-off-the-phone type, but I am glad I took this chance. As soon as I said it, my RP erupted into song, singing:

O say can you see by the dawn's early light
What so proudly we hailed at the twilight's last gleaming
Whose broad stripes and bright stars through the perilous fight
O'er the ramparts we watched, were so gallantly streaming?
And the rocket's red glare, the bombs bursting in air
Gave proof through the night that our flag was still there
O say does that star-spangled banner yet wave
O'er the land of the free and the home of the brave!

As she sang, I thought, *What is happening right now?* My eyes widened and my jaw dropped. I briefly considered hanging up, but my mom taught me better than that. I muted my phone to conceal my laughter, shock, and disbelief.

My son was five years old at the time, so I had mastered the supportive mother's "that's great, buddy!" response to anything and everything he "showed" to me, including drawings or Lego buildings. As my RP hit the final high note, I instinctively declared, "Very nice!" then smacked my forehead with my palm.

The recording of this bizarre call was played over and over and over, and every time, the room erupted into hysterical laughter. My supervisor at the time saved a copy on his computer so that he could listen to it whenever he needed a good chuckle. The recording even received a place within our training materials to teach our new telecommunicators to expect the unexpected. For me, this impromptu serenade taught me to say "sure!" a little more often.

Lea

A telecommunicator never, ever wants to hear the phrase "officer down." When uttered, the world as one knows it swirls around in a tornado of thought and question. In this moment, pain, anguish, sadness, anger, and confusion explode simultaneously. A telecommunicator internally screams but must remain calm. The officer needs help, not a wet, hot mess with a headset and a keyboard. Deep, steadying breaths help channel the adrenaline into action, forcing the fingers to move and the brain to think. This is the ultimate telecommunicator test.

My first test of this nature came when working the primary radio before my second work anniversary on a sleepy Sunday.

"285 put me with a male out front of the 7-11," an officer radioed. With these limited details, I created a community contact call that showed his unit busy at the convenience store with a citizen. He radioed me a license plate associated with the male, and it came back clear to a silver sedan.

"285 can I get a cover car?" he radioed a couple minutes later.

"289 show me en route. I am a minute out," another unit piped up. My hand dutifully attached his unit to the call in the queue.

"Copy 289 I'll attach you. 285 are you Code 4?" I asked for a status, needing to understand his situation more.

"Affirm. I am on Channel Two playing the name game." He filled in some blanks.

The "name game" is when a subject provides a first responder with a fake name or DOB to hide wants and warrants. Usually, this game ends poorly when proper identification is found, or a telecommunicator can help ascertain correct identification from state or national records, or the subject is brought to the jail and fingerprinted. Checking my call notes, I saw that Channel Two was running the provided name through several databases. Without any valid findings, the telecommunicator was trying different spelling variations and checking some out-of-state leads. I could tell shenanigans were happening.

"289 on scene." This dialogue pulled me from my investigation back to reality where I typed the command to show 289 out at the 7-11.

A few other transmissions from county units filled the radio void until a scream punctured the quiet Sunday morning.

"Officer down!"

No call sign predicated this transmission, and I didn't recognize the panicked voice. I was left frozen before my keyboard, eyes wide with shock. I had no idea who needed help. Terror gripped me. Instinctively, I put the channel on emergency and looked at my radio console for clues about the last transmission. *Hold it together, Lea!* My supervisor must have clued in to my panic.

"What is going on?" Connie asked anxiously.

"I have an officer down, and he didn't use his call sign, so I am trying to figure out who it is," I sheepishly admitted. On hearing this, she didn't chastise me, instead our eyes locked and she clicked into Channel One. In solidarity she started pulling up every call for service, attempting to narrow down which first responder was in trouble based on their assignments. While she checked calls for service and worked Channel One, I went back through the recorded radio transmissions looking for clues. I found what I needed and knew who uttered the officer-down transmission: my units with Fake Name Guy at the 7-11.

"Connie, I found it. It's 285's call." I added notes about the officer down and the channel being on emergency and clicked confidently back into Channel One. "I'm clicking back in. Will you call paramedics?" I asked, taking the reins of the call back into my hands.

"I got you," she replied and dialed for medical assistance.

I overheard her side of the call, and my mind wandered. *Was he shot? Did he get run over? How badly was he injured?* I didn't know, but I knew medics needed to get there fast! I also made an executive decision to call a neighboring agency for mutual aid. Normally, these requests are first funneled through a sergeant. But there was no sergeant on duty, and I knew they needed help, so I skirted around policy and procedure in the best interest of my officer. Before I could start dialing a neighboring agency, Connie volunteered, showing me her silent blessing of my decision. In a moment of clarity and silence in the storm, I prayed for my officer. I prayed he would be OK.

> "292 I'm in pursuit of the suspect vehicle!" This update interrupted my quiet prayer, and my fingers flew across the keyboard.

> "Copy. Direction of travel and speed?" I asked, needing to notate this information.

> "Northbound. Sixty-two miles per hour," he shouted over his adrenaline.

> "Can someone let Denver know about this pursuit?" I hollered.

> "Denver, this is county on Metronet," I immediately heard Allison say. I tuned out the rest of her notification, focusing on keeping my hands on the keyboard and my breath steady.

> "How are you doing, Lea?" Connie asked in the middle of the flurry.

"OK," I said, too busy to say anything else. My mind was going a hundred miles per hour. Despite my mental efforts to stay calm, my body was confined like a prisoner to a chair, using only my damn fingers to lead the charge. This is not how the body is designed to operate when under attack! I should be in a battle right now, not sitting at a desk.

"Keep it up; you are doing great," she encouraged.

Soon 292 shut down his pursuit of the reckless suspect in the silver sedan because they were starting to blow through red lights. Quelling the desire to apprehend the suspect, my officer knew the lives of other motorists were more important.

While he was turning around, medics at the 7-11 loaded up 285 for transport to the hospital five minutes away. Simultaneously, I heard Denver advising over MetroNet that they were now pursuing the suspect's vehicle in their city. I only caught this whiff of information and redirected my attention back to my radio traffic.

Five minutes later I relayed to my officers that Denver police had picked up the trail of the suspect's car. Officers pursued it for a couple of minutes before the suspect crashed in the front yard of a residence and fled on foot, evading capture.

While searching the vehicle, officers located a loaded gun under the driver's seat. *Gulp. Wow.* Luckily my officer didn't end up on the business end of that .38. Evidence in the car helped properly identify the suspect. He had warrants and a record a mile long, and many of his entries stipulated he can't be in possession of a firearm. Now the fake–name game made sense. Law enforcement across the metro area were dispatched to check known residences for the subject, but all turned up empty. One contact advised he had connections to Mexico. Upon hearing this, investigators knew he was on the run.

A few hours later, I got the full story. My officer had stopped at the 7-11 for a morning coffee and noticed the subject sitting in his parked car acting strangely, clearly nervous by the police presence. When my officer engaged him and asked for identification, the subject acted squirmier. The name game ensued. My officer called for backup. As cover was arriving, the suspect decided to take matters into his own hands. The gun under his seat burned red hot in his mind. Only a matter of time before he was discovered. *Checkmate.* To avoid jail, he threw his car into gear. Reacting to this move, my officer reached through the driver side window, opened the door and inadvertently got tangled up in the seat belt. As the car drove forward, 285 got a free ticket to a bucking bronco contest with a moderately priced sedan. The car lurched forward, then suddenly backward, away from the cover car that just arrived on scene. My officer was dragged twenty-five feet with his right arm stuck in the seatbelt as an open door assaulted his head with every flop of the vehicle. Thankfully he was able to untangle himself and barrel-roll away from the fleeing car. Doctors anticipated a full and fast recovery since the majority of his injuries consisted of bruises and scrapes. He was truly lucky, especially considering that loaded gun just inches away.

With this closure, I asked to claim some vacation time and leave early for the day. Connie didn't hesitate to say yes. I met some good friends for margaritas, needing to decompress all the emotions and thoughts.

A week later the injured officer brought "thank you" muffins, and we began a special friendship born out of the fire. Over the years, we continued working together and developed a unique camaraderie and teamwork that was forged in an hour of absolute hell. Reflecting on this scenario, I am thankful to have helped someone that day. This horrible incident gave me new confidence in my skills and my worth in a crisis, which helped me build a strong foundation and understanding of my Channel One skills.

As for the suspect, a reward was issued, and investigators tracked his movement to Mexico as predicted. Four years later, he was arrested in Mexico for sending drugs across the border and extradited to the United States. His trial is pending for local and federal charges. Another point for the good guys!

Lea

Telecommunicators have notoriously tough skin. We don't break easily, and we have dark senses of humor. Really dark. We gawk at pictures of gross things and hungrily devour the dirty details of the calls we take. We have tough stomachs and hard heads. But we each have a breaking point. Generally, telecommunicators care—truly care—about three things: kids, animals, and old people. We each rank them differently, depending on personal experience, but this list comprises the holy trinity of things not to disturb.

My mom had died a few months earlier. I clicked off a call, my hands shaking and hot tears streaking my cheeks. This call had delivered a sucker punch. When my mom was ailing with stage four COPD and emphysema, we moved her to assisted living. She lived there comfortably for two years before the hallucinations started—probably due to the lack of oxygen coupled with the morphine that helped her regulate the air hunger. In her current state and declining condition, the assisted living folks couldn't care for her any longer. They recommended a move to skilled nursing, so my siblings and I found a nice place close to three of her five children. She wasn't happy about having a roommate, but with Medicaid, that is all we could afford. She also wasn't happy about the strict no-visitor policy put in place because of the global pandemic in March 2020. But as her hallucinations became more frequent and intense, we knew we had made the best decision, despite her protests. Talking to her daily, I heard less and less of my mom and more and more of this crazy person who spoke about COVID-19 conspiracy theories and naked people in her room, and who used 911 like her own personal hotline. My mom knew I worked for 911, so I think she was trying to get ahold of me. In her loneliness and decreased capacity for sound judgment, she kept reaching out for help in a very tangible way.

Considering my experience with my mom and the nature of my job, I asked my therapist about when and how I could potentially be affected by my mom's death while I was working. I took a lot of calls from nursing homes and people who were sick.

"It will catch you off guard and deliver a gut punch," she responded. "But the silver lining is that you will have a gift of empathy and compassion to give others from this experience," she offered, softening the blow.

Seventy days after my mom died, at two thirty in the morning, my first gut punch snuck up on me. Not only did this call remind me of my mom, but it severely violated the dispatch holy trinity: Don't. Mess. With. Old. People.

"911, what's the address of your emergency?" I answered the incoming call.

"Uh, yes," a feeble voice started, "there has been an accident on my back deck, and I would like to have the fire department send someone over to see if there is a problem."

"OK, you are at 5500 East Parkview Avenue at Holly Brooks? Is that correct?" I said, reading the landline address information from my phone. I recognized the address as one of our nursing homes.

"I'm at Holly Brooks right now, temporarily," the voice stammered.

"OK, but you are at 5500 East Parkview Avenue, is that correct?" He seemed confused, so I reiterated to be one hundred percent sure.

"Say that again," he said, his voice breaking.

"5500 East Parkview Avenue, is that correct?" I asked for the third time.

"Uh, yes, that is the address." He sounded like Dumbledore from the first Harry Potter movies. His voice was quiet and broke with interesting intonations. I liked him already.

"OK, and did you want police, fire, or paramedics?" I asked softly.

"I don't know. That is what I am trying to find out," he stated succinctly.

"Well, you called 911...," I gently reminded him.

"I know I did, dear, OK," he said with a laugh. "My address right now is Parkview Avenue. This weekend I am back at my old place. My old house, which was bought by a realtor and converted into an, uh, extended stay facility." I smiled listening to his delusion.

"What unit are you in there?" I asked, hoping he knew I was asking about the assisted living facility.

"The room is 3000." I nodded to his answer, glad that he understood.

"Is your nurse there?" I questioned, trying to bring a sense of reality to his situation.

"Yeah, I've got two nurses. Well, they are attendants, and they are both from Africa, and there is a communication problem. All I would like to be done is for someone to go up to the upper deck and check to see if there is a hole in the deck," he said as if this were a totally normal request.

"What is your name?" I suggested, attempting to build some rapport.

"Charlie Minno," he replied with the bravado of an older generation.

"Are either of your nurses there now, Charlie?" I continued.

"Yeah, they are out in the hallway," he provided.

"Can I talk to one of them?" I asked.

"OK, sure. Hold on one second." I heard Charlie put the phone down gently, then I sat in silence listening to him yelling in the background.

"I'm sorry, there is no one in the hallway right now," he said on his return forty-five seconds later. This response did not shock me, knowing how drearily unresponsive nursing home staff can be. Across the room, I could hear my partner on the phone. She was talking persuasively to a staff member at the home.

"Charlie, it looks like we are trying to get a nurse on our lines, too. So give us just a second, OK?" I reassured him.

"OK, good," he said, sounding confident.

"Now. . ." I started.

"You are going to have a real communication problem," he interrupted. I laughed a little with his advice. "All communication is hard. They are both from Africa," he continued.

"Sure, I understand that. What are you needing tonight? Are you needing something from a nurse?" I nudged him to ascertain exactly why he called 911.

"I would like to have someone, preferably from the fire department, go to the upper deck from the master bedroom. I had company over this evening, and they were upstairs, and I took one of the rooms upstairs and modified them. . .you know those old houses. And now I am back in the facility here," he repeated a similar request from before.

"Is that your new place or old place?" I clarified.

"No, it's my old place. I designed and built it about forty years ago." Pride puffed his chest. "Just go out to the upper deck and see if something is outside and. . .and. . .and. . .the upper deck is portioned now. The deck faces to the west." I could tell this house lived like a shadow in his head, never leaving.

"Isn't that the prerogative of the person that bought your house?" I questioned.

"Yes, they are making it into a facility for extended stays, and they are modifying the house. They are making a bunch of single apartments. It will be about thirty apartments where my house was." His sentences started trailing off as if he was losing his train of thought.

"OK, well, where is this house?" I asked, out of curiosity.

"In Genesee. 1000 Genesee Ridge Road," Charlie stated.

"I don't know if the fire department will be able to go over and do that for you tonight, but I am going to send a nurse over to chat with you and see if they can't help you with something else," I offered.

"Oh, OK. Go up to Genesee Ridge Road and as you come up across the top, the fire department will be on your right-hand side, you will be heading west. My place will be one, two, three houses to the left. You will come up on it. . ." he explained before being cut off by another voice.

I could faintly hear a male in the background with a thick accent. The nurse had arrived to help Charlie separate fantasy from reality—no doubt because of my partner's stern persuasive efforts.

"Hey, Charlie? Charlie?" I beckoned.

"Yeah, one of my nurses is here!" he said, ecstatic about the visit.

"Yes, sir. We sent them over to talk to you. I need you to chat with them," I urged.

"Yes. Thank you," he agreed, sounding relieved.

"Alrighty, I am going to let you go," I replied, looking at my computer screen to see how long we had been speaking. Almost twelve minutes.

"Thank you," he sighed.

"No problem, sir. Bye-bye!"

I ended the call feeling completely normal, then unexpectedly, out of nowhere, the unsettled dissonance struck, swiftly and with gusto. I saw my mom talking on the phone with a 911 telecommunicator at an agency just like mine. How long had she kept them tied up on a 911 line? My mind played a slideshow of mental pictures: there she was, sitting in her bathroom with a towel on her head, ranting and yelling, one of her many rampages. She was like Charlie, lost in an *Alice in Wonderland* trip. Unlike Charlie, my mom was well cared for and loved by her nurses. When she would call 911, they would quickly find her and then lovingly tend to her. Marla, Jaqueline, and Amanda were amazing. The more I reflected on this, the more saddened and angrier I became for Charlie. Charlie didn't have that kind of care. My partner had to demand that his nurse go check on him. That is not OK. Rules of holy trinity shattered.

Wet, hot tears streamed down my face as I excused myself. I found a quiet place in my office to be alone, and I began writing this story to help my brain process, but the words didn't flow. Still restless, I found someone to talk to who was also awake at three in the morning. Thank God for Emma, who worked the same shift as me. I'm sure her logical mind grimaced when I sought her comfort. One thing I do know for sure—that night, old folks overtook animals for the silver medal in my dispatch holy trinity.

Lea

According to *The Hotline*, an online mecca for domestic violence resources, on average, more than one in three women and one in four men in the US will experience rape, physical violence, and/or stalking by an intimate partner. Intimate partner violence alone affects more than 12 million people every year.[4] Domestic violence (DV) differs from any other disturbance because of the intimate relationship between the parties involved. During my career, not a day went by when I didn't triage a domestic violence call for service. What makes this so prevalent? Well, have you ever been in love? Lust? Cheated on? Those all-consuming emotions are strong and should not be taken lightly. I consider myself clearheaded and a good communicator, but even I can lose my temper and fight with my husband like a petulant child.

A few DV calls to my center live in infamy. Once an irate male broke into his ex-girlfriend's bedroom at five in the morning and tried to slash her and her new lover with a machete. Thankfully, this serial killer–style attack only injured the new lover and scared them both half to death. My units took the parties to the hospital for a full medical workup, a quick police report, and a visit with our victim's advocate folks. The VA pleaded with the couple to stay in a hotel for the evening and find another living situation. The couple insisted they were more comfortable in their home. Later that same day, pissed that the job wasn't finished, the angry ex returned to the apartment with a shotgun and attacked the ex-girlfriend and her new lover again. While the female lived, the lover wasn't as fortunate. After this attack, the angry shotgun-wielding ex fled, a manhunt ensued, and by the end of the day a neighboring agency had him in custody on a murder warrant.

Similarly, a female called into dispatch one night and advised her ex had been sending her threatening texts all night and told her that he was going to come to her residence. She had a restraining order against him and would be arriving home from work shortly. She asked police to come and clear the residence for her and make sure that her ex wasn't inside. They showed up and cleared the apartment. No signs of the ex. While talking with the female about the texts, they determined that a restraining order violation had occurred, so the deputies remained on scene to obtain a written statement. Just then, *boom! bang!* Someone outside was trying to kick the door down. Deputies opened the door and announced themselves with enough time to see an unknown male flee down the stairs. A fight ensued at the bottom of the staircase. During this fight, a hatchet fell out of the suspect's pants. Seeing this weapon and the threat it possessed, police promptly tased and detained the suspect.

Of course, it was none other than the female's ex-boyfriend with not only a hatchet, but also a hunting knife and a meth pipe in his pocket. I hate to think of what would have happened if she hadn't called.

Another call one warm summer night tested my intuition when an all-too-familiar domestic violence pattern played out. I had just finished my break and sat back down. It was three thirty in the morning, and the 911 high-pitched ring called out. I answered. Immediately a female on the phone provided the address.

"Send me somebody the..." she spoke and then trailed off.

"Hello? Ma'am, are you there?" I tried to reengage her but only heard fumbling noises, then two buttons were pushed in the commotion. *Beep, boop.*

"I'm sorry? Hello?" I said, trying to gather what was going on.

"Um, I'm sorry. So, we're trying to dial the 611 customer service. It's, um, like giving us some little asshole recording, and I apologize for that," a male voice murmured, attempted to smooth things over.

Liar. I hated when people lied. I immediately didn't like this fool because his deceit directly insulted my intelligence.

"Sir, I need to talk to the other person that called. The other lady, please," I commanded with my best mom voice.

"Uh, what are you talking about?" he deadpanned.

"I need to talk to the lady that called," I deadpanned back.

"There ain't no lady that called; that was me," he retorted smugly.

"OK, someone else is there. What unit and apartment number are you in?" I said, trying to advance this conversation.

"Ugh, oh god. . ." The line disconnected as he hung up the phone.

Frustrated with his lack of respect, I made it my mission to send help to the female who called. Using my resources, I first deduced that the call was made on a landline, so I had the exact location. I put in a call for service and my radio teammate promptly sent units. Seeing my call for service, my other partner informed me that she received a similar call thirty minutes ago, but it was just the male on the line saying something about trying to call 611 and how "he was nice," so she didn't put in a call. Intuition can be hit or miss.

Next, I checked the history at the address. A laundry list of calls for service popped up, including several domestic violence calls. I added pertinent data from previous calls for service: names, DOBs, and previous dispositions from our contact with this address. Deputies arrived and knocked on the door. No answer. They could hear people inside but didn't hear any screaming or arguing. They knocked again. No answer. They asked us to attempt contact via phone to ask if someone could come to the door. We called—voicemail. Deputies left, unable to make contact.

Forty-five minutes later a neighbor called and indicated that there was a "big fight" going on, and he could hear a lot of thudding noises and a female screaming.

"Ma'am, I think she is getting beat up real bad. I think you guys were just out here," the neighbor recalled. I pulled up the dispo'd call and entered another call for service.

Units returned to a quiet apartment with no answer at the door. A familiar tango proceeded. No one inside was willing to open the door and talk. If you are thinking they should have kicked the door in, that isn't how it works. In these situations, police units' hands are tied. The law very specifically states that forced entry is not allowed unless there is undeniable proof that someone inside is in danger. Based on the circumstance, the occupied apartment was quiet each time units arrived, and there was no indication that anyone was in immediate danger. Because the residents refused to open the door, deputies had no right to enter.

After that second attempt, the calls involving this couple went quiet for the night. I hoped they passed out in an intoxicated huff and eventually moved on. This call still frustrates me, though—a call for help that was never fully accepted or acted upon. I am left to hope and pray that she is safe and out of this abusive relationship.

But not all stories end as peacefully. Another infamous, haunting DV story from our call center involved a sad ending for a confidential informant. Our investigators had been working with a female to charge her ex-boyfriend with a lot of scumbag crimes he committed. She had a restraining order and was put up in a hotel in our jurisdiction while she discreetly worked with our teams. One night, the department of corrections (DOC) requested our assistance because the male in question had removed his ankle monitor. Never, ever a good sign. This guy had all sorts of bad stuff on his record, including warrants for attempted homicide. DOC was unable to locate the male. Thinking ahead, they requested a welfare check for the victim of his crimes, our songbird.

Deputies arrived at her hotel room and knocked. They knocked some more. No answer. No noise inside. The lights were off. The room was unoccupied. When reviewing the hotel lobby footage, deputies spotted the female walking through the lobby and getting into a car with the suspect two hours prior. Holding hands. Like a normal happy couple. DOC was advised of these conclusions and asked our agency to issue a BOLO in the metro area for the car and occupants. The male was labeled "armed and dangerous." After issuing the BOLO, my shift ended, so I went home. The next night, I was told that the car had been located the following day in a Denver alleyway. The female was dead in the trunk. Shot and strangled. Her ending sticks with me to this day.

Domestic violence is so rampant and intense that some people will call 911 while their partner is in the room and pretend to order a pizza to try and get help. This is not something I recommend because while telecommunicators generally have great intuition, this could be perceived as a prank. Text-to-911 is a better alternative when calling is not an option, and according to APCO International (Association of Public-Safety Communications Officials), more than 40 percent of American PSAPs had implemented some form of Text-to-911 technology by July 2020.[5] You can check if your local PSAP has the technology at the FCC link[6] or by inquiring on your non-emergency PSAP number. All in all, emerging texting technology represents a fabulous option for reporting crimes discreetly.

I do not recount these stories as scare tactics but rather to start a conversation. Domestic abuse in any form is not OK. Believe that you are worth it, plan, and accept help. If you or someone you know is looking to escape, many resources offer guidance.

Domestic violence hotline: 1-800-799-SAFE

https://www.thehotline.org/

Lea

"**911**, what's the address of your emergency?" I heard heavy breathing on the other line and sat up straight in my chair, poised for a "real" call.

"Ummm, 14291 South Sycamore Circle," the male yelled while another voice in the background screamed, "NO, don't do it!"

"What is going on at 14291 South Sycamore Circle?" I asked, confirming the address.

"My friend is having a panic attack," he continued over the commotion.

"OK. Anyone using any drugs today?" My spidey sense tingled.

"NOOOOOOOOOO," bellowed the voice in the background.

After this came a seemingly long pause.

"Um, yeah," the RP admitted sheepishly.

"What?" I encouraged, searching for more details. Clearly, someone wasn't in a sharing mood.

"NOOOOOOOOOO," the loud voice screamed again.

"Just weed, I think." I could instantly tell this was a lie. A bad weed trip sounds nothing like this.

"OK. Anybody drinking?" I continued along the familiar line of questioning. We ask these standard officer safety questions on ninety percent of our calls to provide situational context for responding units.

"No," he answered.

"How old is he?" I asked.

"NOOOOO. NOOOOOOO. NOOOO. NoooooOOOOO!" a voice screamed.

"Uh, I don't know. Eighteen?" He questioned his own answer. A lie. "Joshua, you are bleeding. Stop!" he ordered, providing me with a name to the ghost yelling in the background.

"Is he bleeding?" I clarified.

"Yeah, he is bleeding," he confirmed.

"Where is he bleeding?" I tried to summon more information from my RP, who was tight lipped.

"Well, um, just a bloody nose, cuts, and um, a torn shirt." He sounded hesitant to answer but was also still significantly out of breath. "Please come fast," he fervently added. We were sixty seconds into the call, and I could hear Jordan begin dispatching units via Channel One.

"Frank 31 can you copy and assist to rescue in Precinct 2?" she asked politely.

"Sure," he retorted, not sounding overly enthused.

"It's going to be 14291 South Sycamore Circle. An eighteen-year-old having a panic attack. He has been smoking marijuana today. They keep saying he has a bloody nose as well. We are trying to get more information."

"OK." F31 accepted his fate.

"0336." A time stamp signaled the end of the transmission.

"Frank 42, I will cover." A different deputy piped up. Policy dictated a two-unit minimum on calls involving drugs or alcohol.

"At 0336 as well," Jordan recorded.

"Why are you so out of breath?" I asked, cutting to the chase.

"Nooooooo. NOOOOOOOOOO. I WILL FUCKING KILL YOU! Ahhhh, AHHHHHHHHHHHHH!" a high-pitched scream sounded. I had heard this tone before from a fit-throwing toddler.

"Well, I am just panicking," the RP explained haphazardly.

"Why is he screaming like that?" I pressed.

"This is a new experience?" he explained without any confidence. I knew there was something he definitely wasn't saying.

"So just a bad reaction to weed? Are you OK?" I asked.

"I am in no danger," he said, moving a pawn into place, engaging in an epic chess match.

"Just confirming a bad reaction to the weed, right?" I asked a second time.

"I think so. That is what it looks like." I shook my head.

"Alright, who else is home?" I started down a different path, sniffing for more information.

"Me, my dad, and my sister," he said with a chorus of screaming in the background.

"OK, I have help on the way. What is your name?"

"Joshua, Joshua, Joshua! CALM DOWN. Joshua. CALM DOWN!" a new voice hollered in the background.

"Garrett," he answered.

I confirmed his phone number and continued instructing him.

"OK, Garrett, I am going to transfer you to the paramedics so they can give you some advice for Joshua since he is bleeding and having a bad reaction to the drugs, OK? They are already on the way, so just hold tight for me." Even though police units were still responding, I figured this was the best course of action so that Joshua could get some medical help. I initiated the transfer and announced the call to my medical partner at a sister PSAP.

Transfers always involve the repetition of information. Each PSAP has standards to confirm the location and phone number of every caller, much to caller's dismay and consternation. Unfortunately, if policy and procedure aren't followed, then lawsuits are imminent.

"What's going on there?" the new medical telecommunicator asked.

"Um, my friend is having a bad reaction to something," Garrett explained while I continued to listen in and gather pertinent updates. "He is having a panic attack. And breaking things and attacking my dad." *Wait, what?* My jaw dropped. I had been on the phone with Garrett for three minutes (in 911 world, that is a lifetime), and he had failed to mention this tidbit. *Ugh!*

"NOOOOOOOOOOOOOOOO." Joshua again. He was getting really annoying.

"He is bleeding, he tore his shirt, he is hurting my dad," Garrett said, starting to cry.

"Are they fighting right now?" rescue asked.

"Um, yeah," he said, breathing heavily again. With this information, I changed my call type to "disturbance" and gave Jordan on Channel One a heads-up. I also called rescue to let them know the police were responding. My rescue partners assured me that they would "standby," indicating that units were planning to wait around the corner until the scene was determined safe.

"Frank 42, is the male that is bleeding conscious and breathing?" a deputy asked to clarify what he was reading on his car computer.

"Affirm. And now RP is crying and saying that the party on drugs is fighting the dad," Jordan added.

"OK. Code 3," F42 declared.

"Frank 20 copy?" Jordan asked a patrol sergeant. Per policy, a sergeant has to "copy" every code run to ensure it is appropriate. In this instance, because of the physicality of the situation, it is considered a threat to life that justifies a lights and sirens response.

"Yeah," the sergeant approved.

"0338," Jordan concluded the transaction.

"Can you guys get away from him?" the medical telecommunicator suggested.

"Um, yeah. Dad, dad—you gotta get away," Garrett said through tears. "The paramedic! He says to get away. You need to hurry, HURRY!" he squeaked urgently. Then a scream pierced the cadence of the call.

"Tell me exactly what he is doing," the telecommunicator commanded.

"Oh my god…" Garrett gasped.

"Garrett, tell me what is going on." Great move to use the first name of the caller to get his attention and ground him to reality. Classic. This telecommunicator was seasoned.

"He and my dad are fighting. The front door handle got knocked off," he added.

"Is there any other way inside the house?" the telecommunicator asked about points of entry.

"Yeah, the back and the garage door. I can open them," Garrett offered.

"Go and do that now." These instructions were simple, yet manageable. Another seasoned touch.

Only heavy breathing filled the phone line.

"County, are you still with me?" the rescue telecommunicator asked me.

"Yes," I chimed in.

"Garrett, are you still in the house?" he added in his roll call.

"I'm in the garage," Garrett noted. I included this nugget in my narrative for my units.

"Are there weapons in the house?" Great question. I forgot to ask this for officer safety. I silently chided myself.

"Yeah, not on the same floor. In the kitchen," Garrett said.

"Kitchen knives? No guns then?" rescue alluded.

"Not that I know of," Garrett added.

"Frank 31 and 42. Parties are still fighting, and they opened the garage door," Jordan updated the responding units.

"OK," F42 acknowledged, sirens peppering his transmission.

"0345."

"What are they doing now?" rescue asked to gain an update. Just then I heard a sliding door open and shut. "I know you are upset but you have to tell me about what is going on. What part of the house are they fighting in?" rescue implored, having a hard time getting information from Garrett as well.

"Uh, my parent's room," he offered.

"NO. NOOOOOOOOOO. NOOOOOOOOOOOO."

"Oh my god!" Garrett cried.

"Are they still fighting? Is that upstairs?" rescue clarified.

"Yeah, upstairs. They are still fighting. Oh my god! Please hurry," Garrett pleaded.

"I have a lot of help coming to you. Tell me what is going on." The telecommunicator encouraged him to keep talking and giving information.

"My dad has him on the ground, he is bleeding. A LOT! Like a lot," Garrett reiterated.

"Where is he bleeding from?" rescue demanded, offering a steady voice in a chaotic situation.

"From glass. Glass. He got cut from glass." A swing and a miss. "With the glass. . .Um, he tried to jump out the window," he clarified. I balked as this situation escalated to a dumpster fire of poop.

"OK. Is your dad holding him down?" rescue simultaneously asked and suggested.

"Yeah, yeah. He is still bleeding badly," he reiterated.

"It's OK if he is bleeding right now; we just want to make sure he is conscious and breathing," rescue added to calm him.

"Yeah, my dad is OK," he noted.

"I am sending a lot of help to you, and I will stay on the phone until we arrive. But only watch—don't get involved, OK? I don't need you getting hurt too," rescue instructed.

"AWWWW NO, GOD NO."

"Joshua, stop," Garrett said, clearly sick of his friend's shenanigans.

"Garrett don't get involved. He is going to keep yelling as long as he is restrained, OK? I need you to calm down," rescue advised, sensing Garrett's temptations.

"Yeah," Garrett said in between a few steadying breaths. "But he is bleeding A LOT!"

"OK, we can't do anything about that until help comes. I need you to just keep your distance. Where is he bleeding from?" The questions continued.

"It looks like his face? Dad, where is he bleeding from?" Silence filled the line for a brief minute. "He can't tell. How close are you?" Desperation saturated his voice. I checked my AVL map. Units were close. It had been almost five minutes since the call came in.

"Garrett, help is coming as fast as they can with lights and sirens. We are on the way," the telecommunicator reassured.

"I don't want him to die!" Garrett screamed.

"We are going to watch him. Is your dad still holding him down?" Rescue focused Garrett on the situation to provide awareness.

"Yeah," he reassured.

"OK, how old is your friend?" the telecommunicator asked.

"Fourteen? Fifteen?" The truth spilled out. "Joshua? Oh my god!" he cried again.

"I know it is scary. At this point we are doing everything we can. I just want you to let me know everything that is happening." Rescue attempted to steady his wavering confidence evident by his panicked heavy breathing.

"Garrett, I need you to slow your breathing down. OK?" Rescue triaged Garrett for a panic attack and shock. Garrett acquiesced with a few good, deep breaths. Rescue resumed questioning after Garrett's breathing steadied.

"How old are you?"

"Fifteen." My heart sank. Fifteen-year-olds doing drugs. They should be playing pickup basketball and drinking Mountain Dew.

"Is Joshua still awake and breathing?" rescue asked.

"Yeah, yeah. He is still moving," Garrett confirmed.

"OK. You said it was a reaction. Just marijuana, or did he take something else?" My ears perked up hearing this question.

"I am not sure."

"Let me know when the cops are with you," rescue continued, preparing Garrett for the upcoming change of pace.

"OK," he said, working on his breathing.

"Are you still looking at Joshua? Is he changing color?" rescue assessed.

"NOOOOOOOOOOOOOOOOO. NO!"

"Joshua, stop!" Garrett yelled.

"Garrett, let him yell at you. If he is yelling, he is breathing." Rescue sounded relieved.

"I just don't want him to hurt my dad!" he screamed.

"I don't want that either. Does your dad look injured? Still holding him down?" Two questions in one swoop—a risky move for someone in shock.

"He looks OK," Garrett said through heavy breathing. I knew he would only answer one of the questions.

"NOOOOOOOO NO NOOOOOO!" Joshua continued to holler, seemingly aware of the change of pace. Soon I heard additional faint male voices in the background. They were authoritative. I checked my AVL map and confirmed that units were on scene.

"42 coming on scene," he announced.

"Channel One is on emergency for 42 at 0350." Jordan initiated emergency traffic for this call to help responders focus on the volatile situation inside.

"Garrett, is that the police?" Rescue picked up on the voices as well.
"Rescue, we are on scene," I chimed in after Garrett didn't answer.
"Thank you very much," he said.
"Thank you," I finished before we disconnected.

"31 out," a cover unit advised as they pulled up to the house.

"0351."

"42 step up the cover! I'm in a fight!" he yelled.

"0352," the telecommunicator replied calmly.

"Frank 20, Frank 21 is on the way." The sergeant stepped in to bolster the police presence.

"0352." She timestamped and checked CAD to ensure that the unit was added.

"Frank 20, start Greenwood," he commanded, referring to the neighboring agency to our north.

"At 0352," Jordan timestamped. I overheard this request and told Jordan I would make the call so she could keep her focus on the radio. I asked for emergent cover and Greenwood obliged, sending two officers.

"42," he keyed up, catching his breath before he aired, "Get rescue started up here."

"Are they Code 4 in?" Jordan asked to ensure that the scene was safe.

"Yeah, for the time being." He struggled to take a deep breath, mid-transmission. "I was trying to get handcuffs on, but I need chemical sedation."

"At 0354," Jordan timestamped, and I again made the notification to rescue for her. Rescue telecommunicators assured me they would send their units inside.

Silence ensued. Everyone in dispatch was on the edge, waiting. My mind raced thinking about the scene inside Sycamore. A short time later F42 finally pierced the silence and advised,

"42, party is detained in handcuffs, rescue is Code 4," he proclaimed, breathing normally now. A collective sigh of relief rumbled through the center. Everyone's shoulders physically lowered.

"20 to 42, Greenwood is coming emergent, do you still need them?" the sergeant clarified.

"They can slow down. We are good," F42 advised.

"Copy, I will slow them down," Jordan offered.

"You have 21 coming too; do you even still need Greenwood?" the sergeant asked, trying to tally resources.

"31, we just need one of our guys or one Greenwood unit," he clarified. Uno mas.

"20, 21 is almost on scene, we can cancel Greenwood." The sergeant made it perfectly clear.

"Copy, canceling Greenwood at 0400," Jordan resolved.

"21 I am out," he said, arriving on scene.

"At 0401." A timestamp ended the conversation.

"Frank 20, I am clear of this and en route to 42."

"Copy at 0402."

"Sarge, can you bring a spit hood, just in case?" F42 asked, referring to a mesh head covering that prevents detainees from spitting at first responders.

"Affirm," F20 added.

"Frank 42 did you still need the air?" Jordan piped in, asking if she was allowed to bring normal traffic to the channel.

"Keep it just a second with the other car and rescue here," he decidedly declared.

"OK, 0403," she said cheerfully.

"Did you guys make entrance in the garage?" F21 asked ahead of his arrival.

"Front door," F42 offered.

"Coming in," he advised.

"0404," Jordan copied.

Silence. We all waited. This part of the job is torturous. Not knowing or being able to actively help, thus leaving ourselves only to our imaginations.

While the officers' adrenaline was pumping and their bodies were actively burning the welcomed fuel, our bodies produced the same chemicals, but we could only sit in desk chairs and attempt to calm the fire from within. Every time this happens, our nerves go to the edge, stretched a little further.

"Frank 20, on scene."

"0407."

"Frank 42, you can release the air." He finally gave the words declaring the scene safe.

"Copy 0408," Jordan said, oozing with triumph.

After all my units cleared the scene, I called and asked for the scoop. In this instance, young Joshua and Garrett, both fifteen, were hanging out and decided to try some LSD. Garrett had a good trip. Joshua did not. Joshua, in a drug-fueled panic, tried to jump out the home's third story window, breaking glass and leaving himself bloody. Garrett's dad, hearing the commotion, ran upstairs and inserted himself into the situation. He restrained Joshua, trying to prevent any additional attempts to jump out the shattered window. In the end, everyone was OK, thanks to highly trained individuals aligned to produce amazing results in emergency situations.

While I am obliged to dole out the accolades for the stellar folks I worked with closely, you also deserve congratulations. This chapter provided the first complete glimpse of a horrible situation—from the initial 911 call and preliminary dispatch to the treacherous confrontation, and finally a safe resolution forty-five minutes later. You consumed a full serving of an emergency call interlaced with radio traffic. Seeing this dance come together is exactly how you begin to understand the pace and teamwork needed to masterfully dispatch a call for service. And, dear reader, we are just getting started.

Lea

While this job is very serious—people's lives hang in the balance—and every first responder bears that burden every moment of every day, we also occasionally create levity and have some fun. Radio transmissions can provide some fantastic stress relief in the right context with the right people—that is, people who enjoy life and don't mind a bit of tomfoolery. One of my favorite radio games was "word of the day," which involved working a slightly unusual word or phrase into as many radio transmissions as possible. Points were awarded for the most use from a single person or team—telecommunicators versus cops.

One night the phrase was "sweet muffins." It started during a briefing. A deputy was leaving law enforcement for a career in insurance sales. To wish him well, the shift lieutenant brought in cupcakes. (Nothing says "enjoy insurance sales" more than cupcakes, right?)

"They aren't cupcakes, they are sweet muffins. Cuz that makes them healthier," another deputy smirked. On the heels of this teasing, the entire graveyard briefing room erupted into laughter and the banter began. *Sweet muffins* was then the phrase of the night.

I walked from the briefing room to the PSAP contemplating how I could work that into my transmissions for the evening. Thankfully, I was assigned Channel One. *It was on.* I made a personal goal to use the phrase at least ten times. Rounding the corner into the front pod armed with my headset, the clock started ticking as soon as I clicked into the radio. Patrol struck first, then back and forth we went.

"Is your sweet muffin needing a cover car on that suspicious vehicle?" I asked, smiling with my wit.

"I'll have an extended ETA. I need to go to the substation and get a sweet muffin to lure this raccoon out," a deputy retorted after assigning himself to an animal call pending in the queue.

"I see Frank 21 is going with you—he is a sweet muffin," I said, sneakily advising responding units and leadership that a cover car was en route to a domestic violence call for service.

"Can I get a case number on this? It's for a sweet muffin," one deputy asked with laughter in his tone.

By the end of the night, the phrase was used close to fifty times, one of the more successful "words of the day" I have ever witnessed. Other fun words of the day included *Supercalifragilisticexpialidocious*, *moist*, *bologna*, and *bijou*—the latter being selected after I mispronounced it *bee-jow* in a transmission, which apparently required further humiliation.

Instances like this illustrate the strong, symbiotic relationship between cops and telecommunicators. Each side needs the other. Cops can't do their jobs without telecommunicators, and telecommunicators have no purpose without dispatching resources to handle the problems. The high-pressure situations require both to perform perfectly, which can create a pressure cooker for spats, disagreements, and conflict. Telecommunicators will bemoan how the officers and deputies weren't doing things correctly or were lazy. As a supervisor, I fielded similar complaints from patrol leadership about the telecommunicators. After wading through all that bull crap for a few years, I realized that this relationship offers a built-in lifeline and support. After hard calls and during tough times, I would turn to and talk often with my fellow first responders. The shared experiences create a unique deep friendship and a bond.

I found strong and lasting friendships with my blue line family. One of my favorite photographs, taken just after I had my first baby, encapsulates this bond. The graveyard lieutenant and two of my good deputy friends came to my house to deliver cards and gifts after my delivery. The most meaningful gift, as crazy as this sounds, was a box of Lucky Charms cereal. Throughout my pregnancy, everyone speculated about the baby's gender as we waited to be surprised. One deputy wittily nicknamed my baby bundle "Luckyeech Harms," a spoof on my last name and the breakfast cereal. When I saw that cereal, I laughed and cried. The photo depicts a very tired new mom, glowing and holding a tiny new baby, standing next to three strapping men in uniform. I look at that photo with sincere joy and love for my coworkers. We all sat around and talked for half an hour until a disturbance at a local bar called them all to duty. I will never forget the relationships I forged through fire, truly a tight-knit family I was blessed to know.

Lea

My favorite season is fall. I love inhaling the crisp air and hearing the leaves crunch below my footsteps. The mix of warm days and cool nights is intoxicating. Nothing beats the glow of a lit fireplace mixed with a comfy hoodie and a bowl of homemade chili. This is the definition of my happy place. However, I have very mixed emotions about Halloween, undoubtedly because of the many alarming calls I have taken that seemed to be straight out of a horror film.

Below are a few of the more gruesome death stories in my career. Skip this chapter if you need to!

The county I dispatched for included several affluent areas where traditional policing was less prominent. Their graveyard patrolmen take messages about cars parked on the street overnight and drive circles around a total of ten streets in hopes of finding entitled kids up to no good. In one of these sleepy communities, a woman woke up early one morning and called 911.

She recalled drinking and hanging out with her husband at home during the previous night. Things were amicable and light. As the wine took its toll, she noted her tiredness and retired for the night. Due to his chronic snoring, she slept in a different bedroom from her husband. She advised the officers that she woke up the next morning and her husband wasn't up. This was unusual behavior for her early-bird spouse. As she made her way to his bedroom, her discovery was ghastly.

Sprawled on the bed, swimming in blood-smeared linen was her naked, deceased husband. The comforter looked as if an angry painter with a very wet paintbrush had attacked it. Shocked, she inched closer to the horrible scene and noticed his skin looked like it had melted off. Sheets of epidermis had peeled from his lifeless body. Turning from the bedroom to the bathroom, she found a messy blood trail between the bed and the bathtub, peppered with remnants of skin, as if he started melting away on his journey from the tub to the bed. She checked his vitals—he was cold to the touch, but she still called 911, screaming as she described her worst nightmare. Rescue and police units responded quickly.

My officer on scene told me what was inside was the most disgusting thing he had ever seen. His eyes burned when he entered the bedroom, and a staunch smell of chemicals incinerated his nostrils. Then he saw the blood, the mess of flesh and the remains looking like an overripe banana peel. He knew immediately what had happened. Drunk as a skunk, this man decided to draw himself a warm bath, perhaps hoping to sober up or relax even more. He was too intoxicated and did not regulate the water temperature. The water was scalding hot, and instead of adding a lovely sampling of his favorite lavender bubble bath, he mistakenly poured in a concoction of household chemicals. Sinisterly, several open bottles of disinfectant, bleach, and glass cleaner lay next to the bathtub. Scalding water plus cleaning chemicals equaled a painful ending to this man's story. I can only hope the alcohol in his system helped ease his situational awareness.

Another harrowing Halloween story was a horrible hanging. On a beautiful fall day, a dad took his daughter for a bike ride. He was walking alongside her as she pedaled to keep up—a precious scene! —until his daughter expertly spied a mysterious object in a wooded clearing near the bike path. As she meandered past the grove, enough of the leaves had fallen to reveal a grisly sight among the trees. A body. Hanging. She pointed it out to her dad. Peering intently into the foliage, he didn't see it at first, but then the image became clear. Careful not to get too close, he called 911 and provided the location.

"I don't know if it's real or a Halloween prank! If it's a prank, it's a hell of a good one!" he said, chuckling nervously. "I'm not going near it to test out that theory though," he added.

Deputies arrived and immediately canvassed the area. It didn't take long to find the scene. Deep in the thick cottonwood trees, a body hung from a tree. Initially, units were stumped, too. It looked like Halloween prank. Carefully, several deputies stepped toward the scene. With each step, the stench of decay warned that this was no joke. Finally, close enough, they could see they were in the presence of decaying flesh that had been rotting for months. A poor soul had hanged himself from a tree, weeks if not months before, when the weather was warm and the wooded area was thick with leaves and foliage. The leaves finally fell, and he was found by a little girl riding her bike. Two losses of innocence.

Thankfully units found a wallet in his back pocket that helped fill in the blanks of the story. When they ran the name through the state and national database, it confirmed he was a local kid, seventeen years young. He was entered into the system three months prior as a missing person with a suicidal caution note attached. His report was familiar: teenage angst, depression, and suicidal statements made after an argument with parents, and the teen took off. I've taken a hundred of these calls, but this one ended tragically.

A deputy sent a picture of the scene to all those in the PSAP that day. Our sick and twisted minds gawked at what we saw. It was bizarre. Grotesque. Hideous. And yet, it didn't seem real. The body was strung up by rope from a relatively high branch. Oddly, the body remained intact, despite being in the elements for months. His clothes were dirty and disheveled. His silhouette was haunting, especially because the birds had gouged out his eyes. Most shocking was his elongated neck that stretched his remains toward the ground. Gravity plus the entropy of his decay equaled the elongation of his neck. When he was found, his body and his head were separated by a foot of skin and bones. This sight was simultaneously harrowing and captivating.

I had the picture for a while on my phone. I deleted it promptly after my two-year-old and I were looking through photos and videos together, and we scrolled past it.

"Whaz zat, Mommy?" she asked incredulously.

"Oh nothing, just a silly picture," I said, my bulging eyes betraying my even tone. *Delete.* But I can still see this picture when my mind is quiet.

The final Halloween horror story is a man I refer to as non-Narcan Lazarus. You might know the biblical story where Jesus miraculously brings Lazarus, who was dead for three days, back to life—not only illustrating Jesus's divine capabilities but more importantly foreshadowing his triumph over death. In current times we don't really "see" miracles like this anymore. Or do we? People now can be brought back from death's door by an incredible medication called Narcan, or naloxone. This medication is administered during opioid overdoses and, if used correctly, can counteract the life-threatening depression of the central nervous system and breathing system, allowing the victim to recover from system failure.

Several peace officers who have administered the medication relayed their stories to me, and every story felt miraculous. Each instance involved a subject who had no pulse, was not breathing, and for all intents and purposes, was dead. Less than ten seconds after Narcan was administered through the nasal cavity, the victim gasped for air and was brought abruptly back from a visit beyond the veil.

I have dispatched many "Narcan Lazarus" calls for service during my career. Unfortunately, this one was not a save, but an attempt. In one area of the county known for drugs, gangs, and other nefarious activities, we got a call one night about a twenty-year-old who had overdosed on heroin. The information was aired to officers so that they could prepare for the worst and, most importantly, bring their Narcan. When they arrived, they were told that he had been recently hospitalized for COVID-19. He had successfully pulled through treatment only to come home and start using heroin again. On this night, his roommates found him unconscious and not breathing. Officers administered three doses of Narcan. Unfortunately, this young man could not be resurrected like many before him. I wonder if he might have had a fighting chance if not for the virus and the lung damage that couldn't be undone. And perhaps less heroin could have also helped.

Reflecting on these three horror stories reminds me of why I don't like Halloween. I'm slowly rediscovering my love for the holiday, though, thanks to my cute kids frolicking in costumes. Last year my oldest snuck her and her sister's candy buckets upstairs during the quiet morning hours. My husband and I awoke a little later to find sugar-zoned toddlers surrounded by candy strewn about their bedrooms. These moments miraculously dull the horrifying pictures I remember. Thank God for that.

Lea

Remember the dispatch holy trinity? For a lot of telecommunicators, animals trump all people on that list, especially domestic animals. Telecommunicators love their animals! Cute, cuddly, scaly, winged, wild, domestic, or even rabid. A call involving an animal quickly catches the attention of the entire PSAP. First responders are happy to help with all our four-legged friends, although sometimes it's crucial to remember that in this kingdom, animal instinct outperforms all. Once a lady called about a friendly feline atop a telephone pole. She was very upset when I informed her that emergency personnel would not be dispatched. Frustrated with my stance, she requested to speak to animal control. I was happy to put her in touch with an animal control officer, who reminded this citizen about cats' expert climbing skills—if they get up somewhere, they can get themselves down. A little bit of time combined with a tasty motivation at the bottom of the pole proved animal instincts are superior to human effort.

More intriguingly, in an affluent area of our jurisdiction, a family had a very large pig as a pet. This pig had an affinity for getting loose and roaming the town—so often that neighbors and officers knew and recognized the swine. A simple call to the owners fixed the problem every time.

In the same area, Old MacDonald would be proud to add a great story about a Shetland pony. E-I-E-I-O! On a bright and beautiful morning, just as the sun was cresting from the east, my 911 caller (the first of five) advised me that a pony was trotting in the middle of a busy thoroughfare.

"I just don't want this beautiful horse to get hit!" my RP stated, rightfully concerned. "I have my hazards on, and I am driving slowly behind the horse until you get here," she stated resolutely.

I stayed on the phone to ascertain the exact location of the pony in traffic, and my RP continued to gasp in my ear every time a car would swerve to miss the pony. Each time I winced. *Please Lord, don't let this pony get hit!* Finally, two torturous minutes later, units arrived on scene—stumped and ill-equipped. Thankfully, the nervous pony soon spotted a popular walking trail and happily trotted there instead of the street. *Whew!* This moment of relief was fleeting. Then the center busily engaged in a collective effort to make phone calls to possible owners, local horse stables, and rescues in the area for aide. Soon with some proper equipment, an officer was able to wrangle the pony and walk it to a nearby pasture for safekeeping until the located owner could claim him. Before long, officers appeared in a picture on my phone, showcasing their cowboy skills. Such gratification came from seeing first responders walking down a metropolitan sidewalk with a Shetland pony in tow. I went to sleep that morning reflecting on a pretty awesome day at the office—or rather, the farm!

Another domestic animal story included a lovable mutt stuck in barbed wire. When this call was aired, every available car responded. Even the fire department sent units to help cut the pup out of the wire! Loud cheers erupted over the radio when they finally succeeded. Silly pup, barbed wire is not a good place to play.

Although animals are occasionally dumb, the stupidity of pet owners often surpasses them. I have plenty of stories involving blood-boiling neglect. I once took a call on an eviction case where animal control was sent in to retrieve abandoned alligators from a property's bathtub. Who thought a 600-square-foot apartment was a suitable habitat for a scaly fierce alligator? Another call required me to listen to an RP at two in the morning crying because she let her chihuahua puppy out for a potty trip while a pack of coyotes howled across the street. I became impatient and stern, asking her to repeat exactly what had transpired and telling her why she shouldn't go across the street and try to "save" her dog. I sent an officer to help calm her down, but I really wanted to ask her why she thought it was a good idea to let her tiny dog out in the middle of the night in the company of a hungry pack of coyotes. I spoke with similar disdain to a gentleman who called 911 to yell at me about why we weren't more interested in finding his pet ferret that he let off the leash at the park twenty minutes ago. The world doesn't yet have an emoji for my facial expression while attempting to empathize. Billy Currington says it best when he sings, "People are crazy."

Our undomesticated animal friends receive their fair share of a telecommunicator's attention as well. One day a gaggle of ducklings got stuck in a local drainage ditch. A very concerned mother duck camped out at the concrete oasis, honking and creating a ruckus in vain attempts to garner some help. Soon police were alerted, and the responding deputy earned the nickname "Deputy Duckling" after his heroic efforts went viral on social media accounts. The internet definitely needs more attractive young men rescuing baby animals!

But not all wild animals are adorable. Working my fair share of graveyards, I had many calls involving vermin like raccoons. One call involved an unfortunate commuter who got into her car to leave for work early one morning and discovered an unwelcome guest. The raccoon had entered the car overnight through an open window and camped out, leaving piles of raccoon poop throughout the vehicle. The stunned RP called animal control first, but they refused to respond because raccoons are considered pests, not pets. She then called 911, and my lieutenant meandered to the scene armed with a wire hanger and attempted to coax the raccoon from the car. The barking and hissing pest refused to budge. I'm still unclear on how he managed to get the raccoon out of the car, but he provided lovely pictures for show-and-tell.

Aside from calls about cats and dogs, the third animal our PSAP received the most calls about might surprise you. Cows! Normally these calls involved the heifers being places they shouldn't, like the road. While this might seem silly, seeing a cow on or near the road is always a good reason to call 911—unlike wild animals, cows have no instincts and can do a lot of damage to unsuspecting cars. Aside from cows obstructing traffic, a pesky bull near the sheriff's office often broke loose from his pen. Every time he escaped numerous passersby would call 911. Career telecommunicators had memorized the name of the bull's owner and would quickly ring him to retrieve his property.

The animal stories I most love telling and retelling are about the K9s. I loved all my patrol pups. During the 911 education outings I participated in, the K9 demonstration always drew the biggest crowd. The department I worked for was extremely lucky to have a wonderful elderly and wealthy benefactor who generously donated to our agency's K9 program. Each dog's starting cost is around $12,000, which doesn't even cover the costs of training! These designer dogs are bred to hunt people, hunt drugs, and hunt bombs. Departments typically buy German shepherds and Belgian Malinois, preferably male, non-neutered, good listeners, trainable, aggressive, strong, fast, brave, and sociable.

Throughout my career, I observed how closely dogs often reflect the cues and personalities of their trainers, creating a symbiotic relationship that can be either beneficial or challenging, depending on the handler. For instance, one German shepherd seemed to embody the same high-maintenance qualities as his handler. Conversely, we had a Malinois whose calm and focused demeanor mirrored that of his human companion. Another, young and spry, displayed a need for more experience, similar to his handler. Each dog was remarkable, and their stories and instincts always captivated me.

One of our legendary dogs, trained and handled by a K9 phenom, always got McDonald's cheeseburgers after successfully detaining a criminal. Telecommunicators constantly cheered for him on the radio. He once went on a warrant arrest for a drug-dealer and his girlfriend, who were holed up in an apartment after a police chase. An epic standoff resulted, and the subjects refused to come out of the apartment. The male even advised he was armed. The SWAT team attempted to negotiate, but no change resulted. During that time, a search warrant was obtained to enter the house; however, the situation was determined too dangerous for humans to enter. Cue the mighty and ferocious police K9!

> "John 12 making announcements," the handler said on the radio to record the exact time K9 interaction began.

> Behind this transmission, I could hear a dog barking madly and an authoritative voice yelling.

> A few moments of silence passed and then another radio transmission, "John 12 we are forcing entry." *Bark bark bark bark bark!* peppered this transmission.

> "Copy forcing entry at 2039," I said calmly.

After that moment the door was kicked down and the action started. The stealthy Malinois entered the apartment, found the male subject first, and chomped like a champion. After the bites, the suspect was instantly rendered passive to the floor. Seeing this, the girlfriend freaked out, screaming and making aggressive motions at the dog. Not a good choice. She got a courtesy bite that surrendered her to the ground as well. Soon the K9 had the situation controlled and barked to the handler and SWAT team, indicating they could safely enter. Both suspects were handcuffed without further incident. Swiftly all the injured parties were taken to the hospital for stitches, which is where the photo documentation started. Knowing we love this stuff, the K9 handler sent pictures to the on-duty personnel in the center. *Wow!* I don't ever want to be on the receiving end of a K9 intervention. What used to be a thigh muscle was shredded and needed serious reconstruction. A bite worthy of a Big Mac for sure.

These dogs are incredible assets and friends. They are fearless and will go where humans can't or won't in order to save lives! Need assistance clearing a crawl space with a nesting nasty sex offender? *Bite.* Need help chasing a suspect fleeing over eight-foot fences in the pitch black? *Chomp, chomp.* Drug intervention on a traffic stop that leads to a million-dollar cocaine bust? *Ruff, ruff.* Bomb detection at a large political rally or sporting event? *Sniff, sniff.*

I miss the days of the K9 visits to the dispatch center, petting, playing, and loving on those special pups. And just like every pup

- They poop in the houses they enter, and the handler is responsible for cleaning it up!
- They sleep in beds or kennels at their handler's house.
- They like animal friends, and many of them have dog siblings with whom they share homes. Also, if a K9 enters a home, they are trained to leave other animals alone.
- They are great with children. All the handlers have kids who treat the K9 as a part of the family. K9s are trained to be aggressive on command.

And if the dog is fortunate enough to have survived a full career and retire, they get to retire with their handler. Most live very full and happy lives at home. Eating cheeseburgers.

Emma

My first dispatch center was in a tiny town of 3,000 people—the kind of town where you can't go anywhere without running into someone you know. Working in this tiny town meant friends are also coworkers. My work partners quickly became my best friends, on and off the job. Sharing the experiences in this sick and twisted career, we often experienced highs and lows and inevitably became family. But I never expected to go through tragedy alongside these people. Calls and work aside, my best friends and I experienced a horrific event together.

One evening, my husband, son, and I walked into our favorite hole-in-the-wall Mexican place to grab some dinner. We saw a man sitting at the bar.

"Children are so precious!" he said to me, watching my son. "Family is everything in this life," he added, looking me directly in the eyes. Unbeknownst to him, I worked with his daughter and recognized him from pictures.

"Yeah! Your daughter is pretty great too—I work with Meredith!" I remarked back, and we began to exchange many short pleasantries. It wasn't a long conversation, but enough to make an impact. After sharing the moment, we returned to our seats and had a great meal.

Not too many days later, September 12, I was gearing up to help my dispatch center participate in a sprint triathlon. *What was I thinking?* I competed in the swim portion and performed well for my team, despite no training. Meredith, my friend from work, completed the running section and then traveled to Denver to see her boyfriend at the time. I had to work later that night and, pushing through for the team, I stayed awake all day. When I arrived at the dispatch center that night, I was already exhausted and just wanted to have an easy night. God had other plans.

"911, what is the address of the emergency?" I said, answering the call.

"Highway 135, mile marker 9. A motorcycle just lost control and went off the road. He's in a ditch," a young female replied in a panicked voice.

"OK, I'm getting the fire department started that way. Did you guys stop?" I felt my heart beating a little faster anticipating the answer.

"Yes, my dad is out of the car trying to check on him," she said, still shaky.

"OK. Can you tell if he is moving or breathing at all?" My heart paused with my breath.

"My dad says no," she stated.

"OK, can you get out of the car so I can talk to your dad and get CPR started?" I offered.

"No." *No? What do you mean* no, I thought to myself. At the top of a long list of things that don't make sense to telecommunicators is not helping at any cost.

"OK, can you please get out of the car? We need to help him," I asked desperately.

"No, my dad is saying he thinks he's dead." My heart skipped a few beats with this information.

"OK, so you're not willing to get out and help him?" I confirmed.

"No," she responded.

"OK. Just wait there. We are sending the fire department and state patrol to handle the accident," I acquiesced as the only thing I could provide.

After I received the call, I followed my protocol and initiated a page. Because there wasn't a full-time fire department, all the members of the volunteer department were alerted about calls with text messages on old-school pagers.

I moved on to answer other 911 calls, trying desperately to shake off this eerie feeling. I felt a pit in my stomach knowing I wanted to help more and could only do so much from this side of the phone. I had felt this feeling before. As I was attempting to avoid getting lost in these emotions, I got a text on my phone. It was Meredith. She was asking about the accident on Highway 135, a normal question for any nosey dispatcher. Her boyfriend, a volunteer firefighter, got the page on his phone, and it made her wonder because her dad was on his way home from the beer and chili festival, and she hadn't heard from him. Reading this text, my stomach dropped, and I wanted to throw up. Terror. Panic. Pain. I asked my supervisor to call the state patrol to see if they have a name on the "Code Frank," small town–radio speak for a deceased subject.

"It is him," she revealed after her call. Anguish filled both of our faces. Sick doesn't begin to describe what we felt. Knowing the chain of command, I couldn't say anything to Meredith. The chain of command is important in law enforcement. It keeps information flowing properly and appropriately to both the line-level personnel and the supervisors. In this case, line-level personnel didn't have the rank or authority to share this news; it had to be delivered by a supervisor because of its potency and need for truth. I had to play it cool for at least two minutes, knowing her world was about to change drastically. My supervisor and I called our manager and victim advocate into work. Dying inside, I found myself lying in an attempt to protect the last few minutes of normalcy for Meredith. She was smart, though, and when our manager called, the charade abruptly ended. She knew that an off-duty manager calling her meant her dad was involved. While all this transpired, I still had to work the floor and all the active calls, unable to monitor the worst call of my best friend's life. I worked to coordinate meetings with the trooper and Meredith's family for a more personal and official telling of her father's passing. Already physically exhausted, now emotionally exhausted, I couldn't focus on my work. A couple of hours short of finishing my shift, my supervisor told me to go home. This was the first and only time I have ever been sent home on the job.

Knowing what I needed to do, I made the phone call I wanted to make since I found out about her dad. I listened to her crying for what seemed like hours.

"I'm sorry, Meredith, I did everything I could. I wanted to help. I tried to get her out of the car to at least attempt CPR. I'm so sorry," I sobbed. She revealed what the trooper divulged: her father died on impact, and there was nothing anyone could do. Somehow this didn't make me feel better. He deserved better; she deserved better. I shared with her the encounter I had with her dad a few days prior. I told her he was lovely to talk to, he made me happy, and that he was so proud of her. He beamed with pride that day, elated that he could brag on his daughter to a stranger for just a brief second. Although he was not my father, I hold this moment in my heart.

A few days later, Meredith's brother came to visit dispatch. He wanted to personally deliver the wristband made in honor of his dad. He told me that my actions for his family meant more than he could say. I had no words in that moment, and I still treasure the wristband. Because of the proximity to one of our own, we raised money to buy a blue memorial sign on the highway. Every time I travel Highway 135 and see that sign, I am instantly reminded of this sadness. September 12 never passes without my texting her to tell her I love her. For Meredith and her family, I'm part of that memory forever. Even though Meredith and I don't work together anymore, we remain friends, forever bonded because of this story.

Lea

The word *lunatic* derives from the Latin word *lunaticus*; the root word *luna* means "moon." The ancient world believed that sanity fluctuated with the phases of the moon. Ask any first responder and they will tell you that some truth exists within this myth.

Dispatching during a full moon event was always a special night. *Special.* (Can you hear my sarcasm?) We didn't need to look outside to know a full moon was rising; every month the calls themselves informed us. I never used to believe in astrological signs or moon phases, but after working in the emergency services industry for the better half of a decade, I can assure you it's very, very real.

During one particularly heinous full moon episode, I sat down for my graveyard shift and answered my first phone call of the night.

"911, where is your emergency?"

"Yes, hello. Yes. Uh, I am a pastor. Got a call from my friend, and he say he not feel very good. He say he swallowed like ten to fifteen pills," the RP reported with a thick East Asian accent.

"What address?" I followed up on my original questions.

"Uh, that the problem. I don't know," he quickly replied.

These kinds of calls are the worst; we refer to them as "where in the world" calls. This person could be anywhere, and the resource who is giving me information has no idea where to look. I took out my proverbial shovel and started digging.

During ten minutes on the phone, I deduced a name, age, vehicle description, license plate, phone number, and other personal information about the subject from my RP. I kept him talking so I could multitask and run resources through appropriate channels to gather more information. I started with the phone number. *Darn, no history.* Then I turned to the state system and ran his name. Several males with the same name popped up as potential candidates.

"Do you know his middle name?" I asked as a long shot.

118

"Abraham." *Wow*, I thought to myself. *I'm thankful he knows that.*

I scrolled through my eight candidates, and only one had the middle initial A. *Got you!* I mentally gave myself a high-five.

"OK, I do have an address for him that I got from a driver's license. It's an address in our jurisdiction off Franklin." The address was for an apartment complex, which was not ideal. Apartments have a high rate of turnover, and the pastor had told me his friend was recently divorced, so I was not hopeful.

"No, that is not a good addy. He no live there anymore," he stated emphatically.

"Well, sir, I don't have another place to look. This is the address on his driver's license. I have sent my deputies there since you don't know where he is," I explained.

"Can't you ping phone? I want you to do that. It's why I call 911." I rolled my eyes. *Ugh. No.*

"I can't, sir. He didn't call 911 so I don't have 'exigent circumstances' to ping his phone. It encroaches on his rights." It's a simple answer that a lot of people don't understand. "I am putting in a welfare check for this address, and we will go from there," I reported.

I hung up the call and slouched in my chair thinking about the auspicious start to the lunar evening. Already I had taken a welfare check without an address or location for someone who was attempting suicide. I shouldn't have been surprised—these types of calls plague the center during the full moon. It is, without a doubt, the time of the month when calls of this nature—suicidal folks, mental health episodes—are highest. In my center, we classified these calls as "10-96," a code derived from old cop "10-code," a radio language historically used to disguise what was being talked about in transmissions. Only a few agencies still use this method of communication—currently most agencies use plain English combined with encrypted radio channels to block listening ears. The 10-code for a mental subject or situation is 10-96.

As I perused other calls, I saw a report involving a frequent caller who lives in a group home and suffers from pica, an eating disorder in which a person eats things that are not normally considered to be food. Tonight, she had ingested the elastic band from her nurse's mask. Lunacy, I tell you!

Returning to the previous call, I saw that deputies had attempted contact at the apartment address. Someone answered, but as expected, it wasn't our subject. Deputies attempted to track down a better address using their system and sent a neighboring agency to another possible address for a welfare check in their jurisdiction. No luck there either. The trail went cold, and a missing person entry was eventually put in the system. The rest of the night dragged on, seasoned with the flavor of a full moon.

Several hours later before dayshift relieved my tired soul, I was operating Channel One. At 5:07 a.m. one of my call takers triaged a car accident with injuries. I dutifully started first responders.

"David 51 can you start towards a single-vehicle crash, unknown injury?" I said sleepily.

"51!" my early dayshift car replied with gusto. I knew someone had their morning coffee!

"My RP is a passerby who witnessed a single car crash on the east side of Alabama and Parker, Alabama and Parker. RP stated the vehicle is still in the intersection. We will get Colorado State Patrol (CSP) started and rescue on standby," I offered.

"51 copies, en route."

"At 0518."

"David 51 just be advised it's now going to be a two-car crash. A gray/blue SUV and a white SUV. Airbags deployed and males slumped over the wheel," I amended.

"Copy, I'll be Code 3 from my location."

"Copy, Frank 30, copy code run?"

"That's affirm." F30 gave a blessing for the high speeds.

"Frank 52, I will be en route to that too," the cover car piped up.

"At 0519."

"David 51 on scene. Code 4 for rescue, adult male, says he is ill. Vomiting and such," he specified.

"We will update them," I offered.

"Let them know he is hardly responsive," he added.

"At 0522."

"David 51 copy a plate?" he asked. I took the information relayed dutifully.

"Copy at 0523," I added the plate to the call and immediately noticed the entry blinked red in CAD, indicating a match on the plate to something in the system. I scrolled, ingesting the information. The plate was linked to a missing suicidal person, the same name of the pastor's friend from earlier in the evening. *Son of a gun!*

"David 51 be advised that plate showing an ATL for a missing and suicidal male. I took a call for a welfare check on this male last night. He was suicidal and had taken pills. His pastor called us and wanted to ping his phone. This was at 2300," I shared eagerly.

"OK, well I guess that is where the vomit is coming from. Please advise rescue of this information," he directed. I clicked my phone to call the fire department. They took the update and soon joined us on scene to assess the patient.

"David 51 this isn't going to be a crash. Assign me a case report number and cancel CSP."

"Copy. 0528." While enacting those requests in my system, I speculated this call for service would ultimately be labeled suicide attempt.

The dayshift team slowly filed in, and I was ready for bed. My eyes were tired, but I had immense satisfaction. Not only did I know the ending of a story, but all the loose ends were tied up and I got to help. During the next shift, I read the finished report. Because of the information provided, the subject was deemed suicidal by deputies and transported to a hospital for a seventy-two-hour mental health hold. He survived. I sat in awe and couldn't believe that my shift came full circle with this same subject. What are the odds? Only during a full moon.

Flow

Emma

The psychological definition of *flow*, according to the *New World Encyclopedia* is "the mental state in which a person performing some activity is fully immersed in a feeling of energized focus and full involvement in the process of the activity."[7] To me, this is just a fancy way of saying "in the zone." I have experienced this many times in my career, but one call involved notable synergy alongside a favorite coworker. Like athletes during a big game, we made every click, call, and decision with precision and expertise. Our flow was not forced; we were simply on the same wavelength.

During a beautiful summer in the mountains, an abundance of melted winter snow had produced a full river. While this is great for agriculture, it increases the potential danger for recreation—a river at high capacity flows incredibly fast and can be very unpredictable. Many people don't take the necessary precautions to ensure river safety. Proper safety equipment, such as helmets and life vests, and proper boats, not just inflatable rentals, should always be used. Most importantly, depending on skill level, adventurers should go with a guide or someone who knows the river and can advise when water levels are dangerous.

My coworker took the call. A teenager called 911 advising that her family had flipped their ducky raft, a slang term for the yellow inflatable rafts that are cheap to rent—something that should never be on a dangerously high river because the float isn't heavy enough and flips over easily. The caller said that she, as well as her dad and sister, got to the shore safely, but her mom was still missing. My coworker perfectly followed the procedure and safety protocol for this event. She had them stay on the banks where they were safe. She asked them where they entered the river and where they were currently. She had them assess if they were injured. She logged meticulously descriptive updates.

From this call, a roller coaster of events was set in motion, requiring a lot of coordination between two telecommunicators. First, the patients on the banks needed to be assessed, so we dispatched fire, medical, and officers to their current location. Once those resources got on scene, they worked with the family to determine the exact spot they entered the river, which gave responders a length of the river to search for clues about where the mom might be.

As resources were mounting, the command post was set up. In larger agencies, a command post acts as a central mobile unit for all personnel to gather centrally and organize their "attack" on the situation at hand. Since ours was a smaller agency, we settled for a small setup in a central location. Because high-priority calls require many units spanning all different jurisdictions and specialties, a command post allows everyone to gather for briefings and receive their assigned duties. We started making our phone calls to communicate the location of the command post and let all incoming responders know where they need to go first to get their assignments. We were now dealing with three law enforcement departments, the sheriff's office, the local police department, the National Parks department, the fire department, and EMS crews. All available sworn officers and civilian employees listened to the radio traffic and migrated to the command post to ask how they could help. The longer the search went on, the more resources were required because the likelihood of survival decreases the longer the search continues. We increased the resources to search a larger area because the river splits near the entry point and then funnels into the largest reservoir in the state.

My partner and I established our flow, got all the resources to the scene, and armed them with information about the event and the location of the command post. We even called a helicopter owned by the sheriff's office to start an aerial search. We made at least fifty calls between the two of us, all while keeping up with the radio traffic and other calls coming into the PSAP. I honestly can't remember what else was going on that day. All my attention was focused on this huge call!

We were two people sitting in our chairs and working together, our teamwork perfectly synched. We didn't need to tell each other what to do; we simply collaborated and handled the situation.

After a couple of hours, we had a helicopter in the sky; officers, medics, and firefighters walking the banks of the river; multiple boats in the river; and emergency service personnel hand-sifting through all the banks and "strainers." *Strainer* is a topography term that refers to a suction-like pocket created by debris collected in the river and doesn't allow water to flow properly.

My stomach dropped when one of our firefighters advised that a rescue boat searching the strainers had found her. She had been sucked into a river pocket and was not able to free herself. Firefighters called over several other crew members, and they all worked to pull her into a rescue boat and perform life-saving maneuvers. Despite their efforts, it was too late. A bright, beautiful day for a fun-seeking family had turned into tragedy. They had decided to go out on the river, dismissing their mom's reluctance because the water was so high. She had given in to her girls' eagerness for fun and rented a ducky float.

Hearing this, I avoided eye contact with my coworker. We shed tears at our desks in silence. Telecommunicators have an unwritten rule allowing a moment to process before continuing with debriefing.

"You good?" I turned around to ask first.

"Yeah," she said weakly.

We hugged each other tightly, then returned to our chairs to tackle the rest of the day.

Even though we had been stuck in a room and were not physically at the scene, we both played important roles in the rescue efforts. Our adrenaline pushed us forward through the monumental effort. We had worked in sync, physically and emotionally invested. I only wished there had been a different result.

Lea

I love summer nights when the sun doesn't set until nine, the ice cream truck can be heard in all the neighborhoods, and I can sip a cold beer on the patio. Nights like this were the best while off duty, but on-duty summer nights were anything but. The stifling heat boils the blood and leads to arguments. The all-day drinking takes a toll, and the calls roll in. Summertime multiplies the disturbances, domestic violence, juvenile mischief, and noise complaints. Some centers in high-crime areas refer to the heat as "murder weather." I think that nickname speaks for itself.

One warm summer night, around seven o'clock, I received a call from a mom who was playing with her kids at a neighborhood park. She advised that a bunch of young teenagers were cavorting around the play structures and being obnoxious. *News flash, teenagers are obnoxious.*

"And they are carrying around a blow-up sex doll," she stated. She had my full attention.

"Ma'am, are you sure that is what they have?" I asked to confirm this unusual detail.

"It's unmistakable!" she shot at me. My mind was boggled while typing notes in the call. *Who in the heck would do that?* Teenage boys.

My call notes referred to the doll as a "female companion," ribbing at the ridiculous nature of this call for service. After I promised we would send a unit to the area and disconnected, the chatter in the room shifted to a questioning and joking nature. Was this call real? Who would do that? What if that was your kid seeing this? What is the name of the doll? No, it's not Monica. The jokes just kept rolling, and we all laughed our way through our duties.

Then a most fortunate opportunity arose. The Channel One telecommunicator needed a restroom break and asked me to take over. I gleefully accepted the offer to control the radio with a call like this to air. I strategized. I have to air this call! Not for policy and procedure's sake. No. This is a call that must be aired for its hilarity! Just like the unspoken rules in our center that anything on "Hooker Street " or "the Damn Road" got aired. *Wink. Wink.* This call deserved that status! All my time strategizing left enough time for a deputy to self-dispatch using CAD in his car computer. I lamented what fun I could have had airing that call, and I almost felt guilty—until I saw the deputy was someone I liked and could jest with. Also, his wife was sitting across from me. *This was going to be fun indeed*, I smiled to myself.

"Edward 61," I aired on Channel One politely.

"Edward 61 go ahead," he said with a smile, already knowing what I was up to.

"Edward 61 do you need a cover car on your female companion call?" I asked sweetly, emphasizing all the right words.

"I'll advise for now," he stated through a grin.

Using his computer, he updated his status and location to "on scene" and denied me the chance to embarrass him. *Booger.* In keeping with policy and procedure, but also trying to draw attention to him, I checked his status and got the typical Code 4 response. But other calls on the radio kept me busy, so I didn't get any good banter out of him. I didn't pay the call any more attention until I noticed his disposition notes. In his dissertation, he described his interaction with the juveniles and their female companion, "Betty." E61 respectfully asked them to leave "Betty" at home the next time they wanted to come to a park with younger kids. The teenagers agreed and left without further incident. While his dissertation about the situation was hilarious, the picture was better.

E61 sent a picture to his wife that she happily shared with all of us, and we passed it around, laughing hysterically. The picture showed a beautiful sunset. Dark pinks, reds, and purples painted the sky in a masterpiece. In stark contrast, the forefront of this picture showed a goofy-looking eighteen-year-old. Lanky fellow. Five-nine, one hundred sixty pounds. White T-shirt and worn-down jeans. Black hair, rustled like it hadn't been brushed in a week. He wore a poo-eating grin, his arm possessively slung over a real-life sex doll. "Betty" stared at the camera, her circular mouth and creepy eyes way too open. Her pale plastic skin stuck out like a sore thumb in the dusk. The entire center cackled about how unrealistic the doll is compared to a real woman. I'd never seen a sex doll before, but I was disappointed with the representation!

I certainly would have preferred enjoying that sunset on my porch with a beer in my hand, but I suppose if I had to be on duty that night, an evening of stupid young males (SYMs) gallivanting around with a sex doll at a community park chock-full of little kids wasn't the worst alternative. I laughed until my belly hurt. Thanks, Betty.

Emma

Every 911 telecommunicator needs to prepare for the hysterics and chaos of dealing with people on their worst days in horrible situations. At times you launch from zero to one hundred at the drop of a hat, and occasionally a situation catches you off guard, no matter how much you think you are ready for it.

My time happened at zero dark thirty at the end of a solo graveyard shift. I casually made myself a breakfast sandwich and turned on *Friends*. (Confession: I didn't watch this iconic show until 2015. Yes, I know—where had I been? I have since watched this show a handful of times through.)

"911, what is the address of the emergency?" I answered the phone after pausing the episode.

A male voice on the other end of the phone spoke calmly. He gave me an address. Because of his demeanor, I thought he was just another person who was about to tell me "this isn't really an emergency but. . ." story.

"OK, tell me exactly what happened," I said, matching his calm presence.

"I JUST FUCKING STABBED SOMEONE!" he yelled loudly.

He had my full and undivided attention. My adrenaline shot through the roof. In my experience, no matter how professional you are, no matter how many adrenaline dumps you have been through, your hands WILL get shaky in a moment like this. I remember staring at my trembling hands and mentally coaching them to work! *OK, Emma, breathe. Ask your questions. You know what to do. Get to work!*

After thirty seconds of shock, my brain kicked in, and I began asking rapid-fire questions.

"Where is the guy you stabbed?" I asked first.

"I don't know! He ran off," he replied with less enthusiasm.

"Is he OK?" I asked, experiencing a little shock myself.

"No, he's losing a lot of blood. I stabbed him several times in the neck," he stated casually.

"Are you OK?" I added.

"Yeah, I'm OK. I don't think I'm hurt, but he was trying to assault me," he defended.

"Where are you?" I peppered him with questions for information.

"I don't know. . .I ran to this house. I was at a different house when this happened," he explained.

Phew! Now that I had made it through the first set of questions, I needed to get the cops going! Unfortunately, it was five thirty in the morning, and in my tiny mountain town, officers go home around three o'clock because the low call volume does not justify paying them 24/7. This is quite common for smaller rural departments. Since I was the only dispatcher working, I had to wake up a cop with a phone call—and I needed to put the guy who just stabbed someone on hold! *Ugh!*

"OK sir, I have to get you help. Please stay on the phone; I will be right back." I died a little, uttering these words. This was the last thing I wanted to do.

After putting him on hold, I quickly found out who was working the day shift and phoned him. Knowing he lived thirty minutes away, I braced myself.

"Hey. I have a stabbing for you," I said casually, knowing I was waking him up. While he seemed sleepy at first, that bit of information perked him up a bit. I quickly told him about the call. He was up and out the door as fast as he could and requested that I give the police chief a heads-up. *Great.* Yet another phone call prevented me from talking to my suspect! He probably already hung up after being on hold for so long.

As soon as I disconnected, I dutifully called the chief and added another groggy wake-up call. I felt so bad but didn't have another option. Not two minutes later, I was back on the line with the suspect to ask more questions.

"OK, I'm back with you," I said while simultaneously picking up the phone.

"Where are you guys?! It's been like thirty minutes!" Callers in shock often lose all sense of time—telecommunicators learn this in Emergency Medical Dispatching classes. I resisted the urge to reason with him—this was a fight no one needed at the moment. I chose instead to reassure him.

"Sir, we are coming as quickly as possible," I offered. This was not an answer he liked or could even process, but it was the only one I had.

Through further questioning, I learned that this story involved multiple layers and three crime scenes. The stabbing happened at an initial location, then the suspect ran around the neighborhood, banging on doors to get help. At the same time, the victim ran in the opposite direction, also banging on doors and looking for help. Keeping track of these important details to relay to my officers was starting to get a *little* complex. In between all the wild particulars, my suspect gave me a muddy story of how he stabbed the victim in self-defense. The jury was still out on that. Meanwhile, another 911 rang in.

"911, what is the address of the emergency?"

"Well, I'm in my car. An acquaintance of mine knocked on my door and he's covered in blood." I knew this had to be my victim. "I'm on my way to the hospital," my good Samaritan relayed.

I found myself in the middle of a game of telephone ping-pong. I asked this new caller several questions and deduced that the victim was currently conscious and breathing but losing a lot of blood. They were headed to the hospital in a white sedan. I told him I would call the hospital, let them know they were coming, and give them an ETA based on his location. He thanked me for the help, and we disconnected.

Knowing a few things about this situation, I made an executive decision. Typically, my policy and procedure dictated that I page the volunteer fire department for a victim in this scenario. However, this victim would arrive at the hospital before I could even page the volunteers. And knowing there were no cops on the road for speed enforcement, he had a pretty quick and straight shot! My freelance decision paid off.

Just after this call, the officer hopped on the radio advising he was responding with lights and sirens. Because of the serious call nature, I aired an update on the regional channel, like MetroNet, which broadcasts to an entire region for area awareness.

"403 please respond to the address on Elm Street where the suspect of the stabbing is located. Be advised the victim was found by a good Samaritan and is headed to the hospital in a POV. 403 also be advised we have other callers on the phone stating they had a guy covered in blood knock on their doors. They were advised to

not touch it, and someone would be in contact with them," I aired
to advise all listening ears simultaneously.

"403 to dispatch," my unit keyed up, panic coating his voice.

"403 go ahead," I raised.

"Can you call 401 and let him know about this?" he asked,
referring again to the chief's notification.

"403 yes sir, he has been advised," I stated, hoping that eased him
a little.

Within thirty seconds of hearing this message on the regional channel,
my husband (an on-duty police officer for a different jurisdiction) and his
partner came walking into the dispatch center in disbelief of what they were
hearing on the radio. They looked at me like my hair was on fire and needed
to be extinguished. Unfortunately, they couldn't respond to the call because
it was not within their jurisdiction, and they were a good forty-minute drive
from where this happened. However, I did enlist my husband to talk to the
suspect while I coordinated all the moving pieces, throwing other phone
lines on hold and focusing on the radio transmissions. After I hooked him
up to a console, he calmly talked to the suspect for thirty minutes. What an
absolute godsend!

Dawn was breaking, and the workload continued to burgeon. I had
several callers on hold, the majority of whom reporting that an unknown
subject was covered in blood and banging on their door. I couldn't
distinguish whether they were referring to the victim or the suspect since
both were covered in blood and banging on doors. I advised all callers not
to clean up anything and to wait for officers to talk to them because their
house was part of a large crime scene. I added each address and correlating
contact information to the call for documentation. Investigators would need
this information to pinpoint important locations in a crime scene that now
spanned an entire neighborhood.

In this chaos, I remembered to call the hospital and give them a heads-up
about what was rushing towards them. Having an officer talk to my hysterical

suspect was all the help I needed to coordinate the rest of the logistics and resources and to field the other calls that fleshed out the complete scope of the situation. In hindsight, having a police officer talk to the suspect was probably better than me. His knowledge about investigations, suspect behavior, and interrogations proved very helpful on the recorded line. He was able to obtain a full confession for the other police department, making their job a heck of a lot easier. Case closed.

Telecommunicators' responsibilities are often a mystery to first responders and to the public. We coordinate, we delegate, and we work hard to get as many things done in as little time as possible, even if our hair is on fire. Who is the hysterical one? Me or the suspect? Depends on the day. The hour. The call.

Wall of Fame and Fabulous

Lea

Being a fun-loving "yellow" supervisor, I was known to encourage fun and tomfoolery when appropriate. I always understood that the taxing job necessitated a healthy amount of frivolity, and pranks often accomplished this goal. Around April Fool's Day, I was often the one putting tape over the mouse wheel, putting sugar packets in water cups, or hiding toy spiders in desk drawers. My supervisor once retaliated by sending me on an epic scavenger hunt around the PSAP to recover my water bottle after I messed with him one too many times. Joking around about the stuff we saw, heard, and experienced also infused fun into the center. In the business, we would often remark, "you can't make this shit up!" This is the truest thing I learned during eight years of working in emergency services. Every time you think you have seen it all, you pick up the phone and *boom*, something new and crazy happens.

This happened so often that I created a wall dedicated to the weird and bizarre things our telecommunicators discovered. I called it "The Wall of Fame and Fabulous." After any call involving something asinine, crazy, or funny, I encouraged a printout for the shrine. By the time I left, the wall was full of many things that made us raise our eyebrows, giggle, and ugly cry. Each told a story. I dedicate this chapter to the wall and the many memories it held. RIP.

"Inquisitive Adam from Indiana," as he was called, was a jovial character and one of the first additions to the wall. His stunning driver's license (DL) photo showcased a flaming mop of red hair atop his head, reminiscent of Scooby Doo's lovable oaf, Shaggy. Amusingly, in his photo one eyebrow was raised dramatically, creating a comedic effect. I'm sure that was just a typical randy day for this lad, high as a kite. One evening, Adam joined the mass of tourists who have visited Colorado for its generous marijuana laws. Most arrive, rent their crappy hotel rooms, smoke or ingest their weed, get stoned, and wake up fine. Others sit in their itty-bitty hotel rooms, high as kites, and fall out of third-story windows. Poor Adam. He was OK, I think.

Bertha, also a redhead, was another DL favorite. Bertha was about sixty years old when she started her relationship with the sheriff's department. She appeared to be one of the ladies who religiously visited her hairdresser once a week for styling. Looking at her, I imagined my own grandmother. Granny Bertha was extremely drunk leaving Olive Garden one night. The hostess, witnessing her drunkenness, called 911 to advise that she was in no condition to drive. Deputies quickly arrived on scene and found Bertha sitting in the driver's seat, ignition on and ready to go. When they began talking with her, they immediately smelled the pungent odor of alcohol on her breath. After obtaining her consent for a roadside test, two deputies started the routine. Fifteen seconds in, Bertha was already failing. She couldn't walk straight. She asked to take her shoes off. She was a hot mess, all over the place. Finally, during the Horizontal Gaze Nystagmus (HGN), otherwise known as the "follow-my-finger" game, Bertha got frustrated and grabbed the deputy's finger and LICKED IT! He jumped back in shock as everyone else on scene stifled their laughter. Suffice it to say that had never happened before. *Wow, just wow.* Bertha's picture on the wall forever memorialized this radical roadside test.

The wall also featured a slew of before and after meth photos, an entertaining showcase of the truly terrible effects of this deadly drug. If a picture is worth a thousand words, my office had twelve thousand words screaming at me to stay far, far away. I welcome anyone considering this path to google some photos. Meth: not even once.

Various documents on the wall also told some crazy stories, like the BOLO announcement from a northern agency in the metro area. This northern agency got into a little scuffle with some Hell's Angels, the infamous hard core biker gang, and gunfire was exchanged. Their BOLO let the metro area know about this rowdy group and their interaction in case other incidents popped up. On this night in the PSAP, my team and I were finishing the season finale for *Sons of Anarchy*. Reading the BOLO on Channel Two, I cackled at the irony and printed the BOLO as a memento, tagged it with an *SOA* crimson "A," and stuck it proudly to the wall.

Another character named Zebula, a twenty-something-year-old graveyard gas station attendant in our rougher area of town, provided my team endless entertainment. I first interacted with Zebula when he called

911 several times in the same night to report multiple shoplifting incidents in his store. Area vagrants were surreptitiously shopping inside the Shell station and quickly grabbed beer from the coolers then ran out the door. Passing by the attendant, one shoplifter made sure to grab a few Twinkies for the road. I answered the 911 call and dispatched first responders. A few hours later the thieves returned.

"Wait, Zebula, it happened again?" I questioned incredulously on the emergency line.

"*Ciao*! Yes, me again. The same people were just in here and they took more pastries!" he said very seriously. I giggled thinking gas station Twinkies hardly qualify as delicacies.

"Just confirming, you are at the Shell station at Parker and Alabama?" I said, stifling my laughter.

"That is me," he proudly said.

"They are on their way back out for another report," I assured, then continued asking pertinent questions.

This night began months of entertaining calls from Zebula. Unlike other repeat callers, when Zebula called, no one minded. Perhaps it was his charm or his absolutely amazing eccentricities. We quickly deduced that he was a total surfer dude. He elongated every word and sounded like Kelso from *That 70s Show*. He also liberally described non-expiring sweets as "pastries," and instead of saying goodbye, he would conclude his call with a pleasant "*ciao!*"

Intrigued to know more about this character, I asked my deputy who worked in Zebula's precinct for an inside scoop. He confirmed our suspicions and informed us, "He's a total Sk8er boi from Minnesota," and with a spot-on surfer-dude impression, added, "Bruh, I wouldn't even call, but my manager wants me too. . .dar har har, *ciao!*" Zebula was a graveyard gas station legend, which earned him a top spot on the wall!

But the winner of the wall belongs to a stellar Safe2Tell report. As Emma already described, this anonymous reporting system is for kids in school. In theory, this system is brilliant. Students can report drug use, physical or emotional abuse, and suicidal threats in a judge-free zone. In reality, every report was merely a tattletale's dream. More often than not, law enforcement resources are spent sifting through claims to deduce truth from hogwash.

During one graveyard shift in 2016, the center got a tip about a local middle school that read:

"A pregnant spider of unknown species was released into the school building after being kept in a locker all day. The species is unknown, so there is no way of telling whether this will harm students or not."

Wow. I had so many questions. A favorite deputy of mine joked with us about this tip all night. I am pretty sure I peed in my pants from laughing so hard as he energetically reenacted the Safe2Tell tale in a middle schooler's voice, using the word "egg sack" way too many times. Did I mention that telecommunicators like to have fun? We will leave it at that.

Lea

Suicides are prevalent and represent the worst calls a telecommunicator will ever take. It is heartbreaking and gut-wrenching to listen to loved ones discover a significant other, brother, sister, friend, or family member have made the most permanent choice.

During my career, I had my fair share of these calls. Hanging, pills, gunshot wounds, circular saw. I once thought suicide was for the weak, a remembrance that now makes me shudder. Only through my own struggle with suicidal thoughts and battles with depression have I come to truly empathize with those who are in great need. When my second baby was six months old, my schedule switched to the night shift, and I decided it was time to wean my little one. The combination of the sleeplessness and the hormone shift brought me face-to-face with very dark thoughts. I recall the whispers and sinuous lies creeping in on me during quiet moments. *I wasn't worth anything. I was a burden on my family. I should just kill myself.* I vividly recall fantasizing about tying a noose to my banister and hanging myself or driving my car through a telephone pole. It was the scariest situation I had ever experienced to date.

I knew I needed help. Realizing I couldn't do this myself—always a downer for a type A high achiever—I lay on my closet floor and explained these thoughts to my husband. Through tears, we made a plan. I began taking medication, continued to talk to my therapist, and worked through the darkness. Afterward, I was rewarded with a lot more empathy for folks who suffer. Sometimes you can't help it, and there is a chemical imbalance that causes the nastiness. Sometimes it's about surroundings and self-talk.

If you or someone you love are in crisis, call 911 or the National Suicide Prevention Hotline (800-273-8255) for immediate help.

Every telecommunicator vividly remembers their first suicide call. What makes the first suicidal call so memorable? Is it the trauma of listening to someone experience the death of a loved one? The realization that you are dealing with life or death? Your caller's emotion? Your complete unpreparedness?

All of the above.

No telecommunicator can "prepare" for the magnitude of their first suicide call. No amount of knowledge about how to work the system, enter calls, ask questions, and triage a tough call can prepare a telecommunicator for the screaming on the other end of the line.

The brain takes a minute to process. *Wait? This isn't a traffic complaint, a neighbor dispute, or a cold theft from a motor vehicle?* Cue the sweating palms and the increased heart rate, the shaking fingers that forget how to type. The brain fogs over and forgets what questions are appropriate. The mouth goes dry and stammers when words try to come out. Time simultaneously slows down and speeds up.

My first suicide call came on a spring day with chilled, crisp air that weighed heavy with each breath. I had been out of training for six months and was working a relief shift when I answered a call and was immediately met with blood-curdling screams. I tried to calm the caller enough to give me an address, but she couldn't hear me. She was screaming at the top of her lungs. Yelling. Crying. Broken.

I froze.

Muttering about needing her address, I forgot to check my phone computer for any data. I was so focused on the screaming that I forgot everything about my training. Thankfully my adrenaline kicked in, allowing me to start thinking again. I typed a little bit but still didn't have an address. One minute into the call and I had nothing to show.

Check the phone, my brain whispered. I looked up and saw the RP was calling from a landline phone. Thank God, a saving grace moment. I inputted the address and titled the call "welfare check" with notes indicating an unknown problem was occurring with a very upset female on scene.

I verified the address with the caller.

"YES!" she screamed angrily at me. At least there was a start.

"I have lots of help on the way to you, ma'am," I offered meekly. She continued to wail. As my ear adjusted, I could hear words repeated in her screams. Husband. Dead.

"Is someone dead?" I asked.

"YES!" she sobbed. Thankful to have a direction and working fingers, I added this to my call notes and changed the title of the call. Responding officers now went Code 3. Fast.

"How did this happen?" I asked next. She managed to tell me between breaths he had hanged himself.

"Do you want to attempt CPR?" I questioned.

"No no no no no," she replied. "It's too late!" she screamed at me, angrily.

I tried to get her out of the room, so she wasn't actively looking at her husband. But she refused. In the six minutes it took officers to get on scene, a lifetime had passed. She continued to wail at me. Why weren't we there already? Where were you? She just yelled over and over again. It was emotional, raw, and personal; my mind went blank again. My brain stopped working. My call notes were on repeat—I think I typed "female screaming for us to hurry up" ten times. In hindsight, during that phone call, I went through every stage of grief with her. Shock. Pain. Anger. Bargaining. I remember anger was the most prevalent. She was so hurt about what had happened, and I was her punching bag.

When the deputies got to the scene and I released the line, I sat at my console for a minute trying to take it all in. Then the tears came. I bolted from my chair, making a beeline for the bathroom. Locking the door behind me, I stood against the door allowing it to brace me upright. I was in shock. All I could hear was her screaming in my ear. *Hurry. You aren't doing enough. You aren't doing your job.* These lies attacked me, and I let them. A knock on the bathroom door snapped me out of this loop. I opened the door and peeked my tear-stained face around the corner. My supervisor stood before me.

"Was that your first suicide?" Connie asked. I nodded. She hugged me and told me to take a minute for myself.

"Let's find some time tomorrow to review this call in my office," she offered before letting me have a moment to compose myself.

The next day I walked into her office, still a little fragile, and we debriefed the call. After asking me how I was doing, Connie then provided the ending I needed to hear. A teacher at a local high school came home from work to find her husband had hanged himself in their unfinished basement. He was cold to the touch and beyond help. He had recently been laid off from his job and was enduring a major depressive episode. Somehow hearing the context helped me digest the caller's total emotional breakdown.

We then discussed call performance. She asked good questions, like why I didn't immediately transfer to rescue and let them handle the call. I told her it was still a tenuous situation, and not knowing exactly what was going on, I didn't want to risk officer safety. She assured me with the information I had, this call could have been passed to rescue for triage. I was hard on myself. She looked at me, confirming the call wasn't perfect, and that I had let the emotion get to me, but it was understandable being my first completed suicide. With that sting, Connie then reminded me that I got help where someone needed it. I did the job. I got it done.

"The next one will go more smoothly," she promised. And it did.

At the end of my career, I answered a suicide call the week before I resigned, and it brought all of those memories flooding back with an eerie déjà vu. I had just completed my administrative duties in my office and moved to the floor. I read through all the calls to be familiar with them. One piqued my interest—a suicide threat in a rural area. I quickly read all the details. A concerned mom reported that her adult son left a "suicide note" voicemail. She knew he was having problems with his wife, and she was very concerned. She gave us information about where he should be and what car he drives. Deputies checked the areas she mentioned and went to his house to speak with his wife. First responders were unable to locate him but entered him as a missing person with a caution about suicidal tendencies.

Two hours later a 911 call came in. I answered, and my ear was met with screaming. Seasoned now from my eight years of service, I knew this was a *real* 911 call. Instinctively I checked my phone screen for the location information while I started typing call notes and instructing the caller to take deep breaths. Details I ascertained from my phone informed me that the female was calling on a cell phone in a rural part of the county. I saw an approximate location and confirmed that she was at a recreational trailhead. While geo-verifying the location, I sensed where this call was going. The earlier suicidal subject call flashed like a neon sign in my brain. Within thirty more seconds of questioning, I learned that this RP found her husband parked at the trailhead with a gunshot wound to the head. He was beyond help. Knowing the next steps in this process, I switched her over to fire and rescue dispatch and listened in as she entered several stages of grief.

These two calls, years apart offered me a mirror. While both illustrate the absolute horror of suicidal calls for telecommunicators, I was able to reflect on my aptitude and ultimately rest in the comfort of knowing that I had provided necessary aid for these loved ones during dark times. The inexperienced, naïve DINK who answered that first call back in 2014 was no longer. Hardened by years of emotional scarring from emergency services combined with the natural maturity of having a family and getting older, I realized I had changed. What is the silver lining? The ability to empathetically listen to a heart breaking because of my own experience with suicidal ideation is a gift. For that I am grateful.

Lea

Early in my career, one of the best perks of my job was having three-day weekends. I worked four ten-hour shifts followed by three glorious days of rest, and then I returned refreshed and ready to get my hands dirty all over again. Before I had children I would spend one day cleaning, doing laundry, and taking care of all chores and appointments. I filled the other two days with socializing, seeing my mom, going to a movie with a friend, or having a date night. I look back fondly on these days of living in a 900-square-foot condo. It was simple but grand, granting me the freedom to have fun and be unfettered.

Slowly this scene progressed, and we bought a house and started a family. My weekends morphed from freedom to family. As a mom of two, my epic weekends evolved from beers and burgers to diapers and Daniel Tiger. In my previous life, I trained for a marathon; my fitness goal later shifted to wearing my kids out so that they would nap in the afternoon, and I could fold laundry without them immediately upending it. I maintained my sanity in those days by playing outside with my girls. Walks. Trails. Bike rides. Playing in the local stream. Going to the park. My daughter used to say "different park?" when I asked her about our plans for the day. We loved to explore and find new places to enjoy.

On one particularly beautiful and sunny day, my daughters and I took a walk in the morning to beat the afternoon heat. On our way back home, I stopped the stroller at my neighborhood park and swiftly unbuckled my burgeoning toddlers to run off some energy. This small park had three slides and one climbing element. I was on top of the structure with my one-year-old when I saw my three-year-old slip down the slide.

"Good job!" I called to her with a smile. She looked up at me from the wood-chipped earth, mirroring my smile. Her grin soon turned to a sly look. Every mom knows exactly what I am talking about. *That* look. Quick as lightning she darted to the stroller. Inside the stroller, I had all the classic mom supplies: water bottles, snacks, tissues, and—most tempting to any stealthy toddler—Mommy's phone. From yards away, I spied her digging around the stroller pockets. *Uh-oh.* I scooped up my littlest one and traversed the levels of the play structure as quickly as I could, somewhat akin to my Tough Mudder days. Meanwhile, my threenager had a firm grasp on the magical device. Like Harry holding the Marauders Map at midnight, she was up to no good!

Just then everything moved in slow motion. I released my one-year-old onto the playground mulch and swiftly moved toward the little traitor, but she ran away from me at lightspeed. *Arrrghhh!* I stretched out my arm but was no match for her crazy land-mammal–toddler-agility.

Beeeeep. Beeeeep. Beeeeep. My phone alarmed. I knew exactly what was happening. She had depressed the side button on my device and initiated an emergency call.

I changed tactics and yelled at my toddler to garner her attention. Startled, she stopped dead in her tracks, and standing motionless, extended the phone toward me. Her eyes pleaded *sorry!* and *fix it!* She knew something bad was happening. I grabbed the phone from her hand, knowing what awaited me.

"911, where is your emergency?" a coworker answered. I knew her voice instantly.

"Hi Jaime, it's Lea. . ." I said sheepishly.

Jaime laughed.

"Um, I am so sorry, Maybel dialed. It was an accident." I chuckled a little, but my cheeks still flushed with embarrassment.

"Oh, no worries!" Jaime said with a perky tone.

"Maybel, do you want to say hi to 911?" I asked her as she cowered in the corner of our neighborhood gazebo. "No? That is what I thought. Toddler embarrassment. I am so sorry, Jaime!"

"Have a safe day!" she chuckled.

"You too," I replied, ending the call.

After my heartrate returned to a normal pace, I called my mother-in-law. We had a proper laugh at the situation and the irony, but I was still mortified. A 911 dispatch supervisor's toddler called 911. A kiddo, playing with a phone, attempting to hear her favorite song, dialed 911, effectively wasting emergency resources and tying up an emergency line. A major job pet peeve.

It's a funny story that got me fifty-five Facebook likes, eight chiding comments, and some major laughs on social media, but it also highlights a real problem for the 911 industry. Children playing with disconnected phones, as well as butt/pocket dials, are incidents that plague emergency services.

A case study published in the *Journal for Emergency Dispatch* highlights this issue. Valley Emergency Communication Center (VECC), serving Salt Lake City and the surrounding area, receives 2000 calls per day. Annually, more than 1 million calls are processed in this PSAP. But here's the real eye-opening statistic: Nearly 29 percent of these calls are unintentional calls! [8] This means close to 600 calls each day are accidental. Six hundred calls! But they're calls nonetheless, and telecommunicators have a duty and obligation to process each call seriously. Each call requires anywhere from ninety seconds to two minutes to follow policy and procedure and to properly vet for callbacks and voicemails. This equates to a lot of manpower, time, and resources spent following up on meaningless phone calls made from butts, pockets, and ornery children. In the meantime, other incoming emergency calls coming into the center cannot be processed as quickly due to the triaging of these other dials.

It can happen quickly. On current Android devices, rapidly pressing the side button five times initiates a countdown to call emergency services; on a current iPhone or Apple Watch, pressing the side button five times will initiate a slider to activate an emergency call, or holding the side button and a volume button begins a countdown to call with an accompanying alarm. So, a phone in a tight pocket or purse (or a toddler incessantly pushing the button trying to change the song) could potentially result in an accidental call to 911.

Avoid this mishap by not putting your phone into a tight space and not allowing kids to play with phones, even the disconnected ones, which still have programming to call 911.

If it does happen, DO NOT HANG UP. The call has already been put through to the PSAP, and if you hang up, the center receives the call as abandoned and is required to call back. If you hear that awful noise, find your phone and be ready to talk to a telecommunicator and admit it was an accidental dial. Stay on the line, explain, and disconnect. Have a drink later to relieve your embarrassment. I think I had a few myself after the park incident. Cheers!

Lea

The average 911 call is approximately three minutes in duration. Telecommunicators get accustomed to this kind of turnaround. Answer the call, obtain the necessary information, and get off the phone. Move on to the next call. This is the expected performance for all telecommunicators across the nation. But every once in a while, you get *that* caller. Not the caller who needs more attention because of the emergency they are in, but the frequent flyers. Picture the worst rewards club membership ever. These members use and abuse 911 as their personal therapy line. They drone on for ten-plus minutes about topics that range from their favorite meals to the loss of therapy rats. These folks need way more support than 911, the police, or even a mental health crisis line can offer, unfortunately.

They are very ill.

I had one such member whom I talked to quite often, approximately every Sunday morning at four o'clock. Through all of our conversations, I learned about his brutal racist attack in Denver years ago that led to his TBI and a resulting mental health crisis. To his credit, he was a nice caller. He was never mean or vile. He was polite and took direction but often just needed to vent. One of his many Sunday morning vent sessions, as seen below, showcases the therapist hat telecommunicators often wear. This particular conversation lasted nearly six minutes on the nonemergency line. I intentionally allowed him to dominate the conversation, providing him space to air his grievances without interruption.

"County Sheriff, this is Lea," I said sleepily.

"Hey, are you a dispatcher?" he asked. I heard a click on the phone line, letting me know he had been blindly transferred.

"I am. How can I help you?" I recognized the familiar voice. Morgan.

"I just spent a long time talking to the other dispatcher because I was trying to get some help from them because I am in a really bad situation. . ."

"Is this Morgan?" I interrupted. I wanted him to know that I knew his story.

"Yeah, but let me explain. I just spent five minutes with him explaining what the problem was. But you know. Like sometimes people don't want. . .The problem is this. . .Like sometimes. . .I am of the perspective that the first attacker can get away with murder. I am of the perspective that if I were never injured, and I was allowed to build up my resources and stock up and like plan, then I could get away with murder. Right? I am of the perspective that the first attacker has the advantage. In this situation the first attacker is the other guy. So, if he comes up to me on the first day and cuts out my eye and cuts my arm off. Right?"

"OK," I said politely during his brief pause. This was clearly not a give-me-feedback pause. As soon as the words left my lips, he continued.

"Well, you know. Do I really trust the group of twelve people to equalize my eye and my arm? Do I really trust a group of twelve people to decide what is equal to my eye and my arm? Maybe not, right? So here is the thing. If he comes up to me—I am not ready—if he wants to surprise attack me, I am not ready to lose my eye and my arm, right? I am not ready to lose my eye and my arm. OK. So, are you still there?"

"I am here. I am listening," I offered after unmuting my phone.

"Yeah, yeah, so, so!" he continued with gusto. "I guess a lady comes up to me on the first day and surprise attacks me, I am not ready to lose my eye and my arm. I am not ready. And so, the thing is people want to argue that if I lose my eye and my arm on the first day that on the second day, now I am prepared. I'm prepared! Apparently, I am prepared in the situation, and that the other guy. . .oh yeah! Now I'm surprising the other guy? That is bullshit!" he escalated, recalling his trauma.

"It is the first attacker. Right? I've already lost my eye and my arm, there is not much *surprise* I can do on the other guy. It's not like if I attack him on the next day, or or or one of the days of the coming months. It's not like I surprise attack him. It's not like, it's not like, it should be of no surprise if I attack him after he has cut out my eye and my arm on the first day. Like, there should be no surprise if he gets attacked in the near future. There should be no surprise to this guy. Like if he cuts out my eye and my arm on the first day there should be no surprise. He is already prepared. He is prepared the first time he attacks. He should be prepared the first time he attacks. So, because of that, because he is prepared the first time he attacks, then he is also prepared the second time. He is also prepared, so if I come up to him after losing an eye and an arm and maybe try and do something similar to him and he says that and he breaks my leg, he comes up to me and he just breaks my leg, breaks my leg and my friggin' teeth and cuts out my eye, breaks my ribs and now he says it is self-defense. OK no. He has already forfeited his rights the first time he attacked me. He has already forfeited his rights the first time he attacks me. So it should come as no surprise to me, he is already prepared. The very first time he attacks, he is already prepared. He is already prepared, he is already prepared. He is already prepared. And so, that is my point that the first attacker has the advantage. The first attacker is going to get away with it. Get out of it. And, uh, so my concern that there are other citizens, there are other citizens out there working with police—I don't know what jurisdictions, but helping the police—that are helping this guy make his advantage, after he surprise attacked me. So there are people, there are people..."

"Morgan, where did all this happen?" I interrupted to give him a little reprieve from his loop. I already knew the answer to this question but wanted to start channeling his thoughts into a more purposeful conversation. He rebuffed my initial request, and then I asked again.

He finally conceded and offered where this all occurred. It was not an agency that I had jurisdiction over, and he knew this. For all his plight, he was a smart guy.

"Yeah, yeah. . .my point is why would other citizens work with police to help him? To *help* him? Maintain this advantage over me after a surprise attack. Right? Like they should not help him because as the first attacker he is already prepared. . .they are trying to argue that after I lost my eye. . .uh, well, you know. . .this is all. . .this is all not exact, I didn't exactly lose my eye, but you know what the nerves behind my eyes are damaged, means I have severe head damage, brain damage, behind my eye. It's pretty similar already, like yeah, so say I have like severe eye, yeah if I lost my eye on the first day. They are basically saying that I am the first attacker. No. I am not, there is only one first attacker, uh, and that guys is prepared. That guy is prepared. What's about to happen? Well, that guy is prepared! " he launched.

I pushed mute on my phone to release a sneeze. At this point, this call had lasted over five minutes—a lifetime for a telecommunicator. Despite my ear agony, I felt for him. Morgan's story was staggered and jutting, but there are strange portions that were incredibly lucid. I imagined this dichotomy perfectly resembled his new normal after the life-altering attack.

Several months after taking this call, I found out that Morgan was arrested for murder. I thought to myself, *he finally got revenge on those who had hurt him*, not unlike Inigo Montoya in *The Princess Bride*. However, Morgan's revenge was not quite as poetic. Morgan snapped in a road rage incident. He was driving near a vehicle with a loud exhaust, and perhaps this loud noise triggered him. He and the other driver got into an altercation while stopped at a red light. Morgan got out, drew his gun, and shot the other vehicle's driver and passenger. Investigators later discovered that the bullets he used were special order, made to pierce body armor. He had been planning revenge like he always talked about. Traffic cameras quickly identified him, and an arrest warrant was swiftly issued. The SWAT team was dispatched to his address, prepared for a fight, but Morgan surrendered peacefully. Of course. The man I had talked to a million times about calming techniques like bubble baths and painting wasn't a killer. He was severely mentally ill.

Morgan's problems aren't rare. The National Institute of Mental Health estimates 26 percent of Americans ages eighteen and older, about one in four adults, suffers from a diagnosable mental disorder each year.[9] Depression. Anxiety. PTSD. Bipolar. There is a new boogie man in town, folks, and he isn't wearing a hood or hiding in shadows. First responders are facing this terror daily with limited resources and very few options for true resolution. What is the answer? I'm not certain. I do know we can no longer afford to keep this escalating mental health crisis hidden in the shadows.

Lea

I was raised around water. I spent summers at a lake, I had a pool in the backyard of my childhood home, I was a lifeguard through college (best job ever), and I have been in three of the world's oceans. I can't imagine life without a nearby body of water. I understand that this is not everyone's experience. In fact, one of my best friends still doesn't know how to swim. This boggles my mind. Maybe you are nodding your head in agreement or thinking it's not a problem. My years in dispatch have unequivocally convinced me that everyone needs swim lessons.

Of all my stories, this is one of the most painful. When people ask me about the crazy stories I have heard, this one always comes to mind, but I don't tell it. Until now.

It was a hot summer day tipping ninety degrees. Like most summers in the dry climate of Colorado, if you weren't near water then the sweating, chafing, and irritation would slowly eat your soul, and air conditioning is your only line of defense. I was working a swing shift, and the sun was just starting to crest the western mountains. I passed time on my laid-back Saturday shift reading a book and answering phones. A 911 rang out, and I quickly answered, throwing my book aside.

A panicked middle-aged female voice told me a little girl was at the bottom of the apartment complex pool. *Gulp.* Instantly shaking, I ascertained the address and dropped a medical assist call for service in the queue. I transferred the call to the fire department, knowing possible life-saving instructions would be necessary. I announced the call to the new PSAP, and muted my phone to listen in.

"We have to go on Dayton," I hollered over to my radio. "It is a drowning."

"Aw, man! That sucks," Talia exclaimed. "Ugh, and a kid!" she added, reading the notes. Immediately the call was aired, and units announced they were responding with lights and sirens. One of the responders was a recruit who had shadowed me in dispatch earlier in the week. I said a little prayer for her, knowing the difficulty she was about to face.

Interrupting my prayers, the RP recounted to the medical telecommunicator the events leading up to her discovery. As she was loading her kids into her van, parked by the pool, an older gentleman yelled for her to call 911. She struggled to locate him, but soon saw he was yelling from the third floor of the apartment building. From his vantage point, he could see the haunting outline of a small body at the bottom of the pool. She immediately rustled for her phone while he ran down the stairs clutching his keys. He was at the gate fumbling with the lock while she was dialing. As she spoke, the elderly male deftly jumped in the neighborhood pool to fish the young female from the bottom. He swam to the stairs and pulled her from the water.

"She doesn't look like she is breathing," the RP recounted. "Her face is ashen." I knew what was going to happen next.

"Bring the phone closer to the patient. We need to start CPR," the medical telecommunicator said decisively.

"Lay her flat on her back. Can you do that?" rescue demanded.

"Yes," she said with a wince.

"OK, once she is flat on her back, I want you to put the heel of your hand on the middle of her chest and push hard and fast to my count. Are you ready?"

"Yes," she stammered, unsure.

"One and two and three and four and five. . ." rescue began counting, intending for him to follow the rhythm. "You need to count with me and pump the center of the chest hard and fast!" they added.

The telecommunicator started counting and instantly the RP's breathing changed with the exertion. Performing CPR is a cardio workout. When done correctly, you should be out of breath, and the sound of crunching ribs should meet your force.

"There's lots of water coming out of her mouth!" the RP offered a few rounds in.

"That is supposed to happen, keep going! Six and seven and eight and nine. . .," rescue continued, unphased.

Suddenly, the elderly male screamed that the police were pulling up. I could hear the commotion in the background as he gave them entry into the pool area. I heard a familiar voice in the background declaring that police are resuming CPR efforts.

The phone disconnected. Later I found out first responders continued CPR the entire way to the hospital. During the commotion, the victim's five-year-old sister was discovered standing and watching outside the pool gate. She had hidden behind some bushes, but when her sister was pulled from the pool she emerged with tears in her eyes.

Police asked her the location of her parents. She was unable to answer, so rescue transported her in the ambulance to the hospital. After being rushed to the emergency room, the victim was declared dead by the attending doctor. Medical personnel tried to ascertain from her sister how long she had been under the water, but the only thing the sister could manage with certainty was to tell doctors the victim was seven years old.

I was off shift and was taking an evening run to clear my head when the news reached me about this death. My caller ID displayed the number of my peer support lead, and my stomach dropped. I knew the news before I picked up. I cried dramatically on the side of the road. Mourning for a family I didn't know. Struck by the tragedy of the situation. I was stunned. Speechless.

So many questions flooded my brain. I wanted to know why. What happened? How could this happen? It took years for this whole puzzle to come together, but eventually I learned the tragic details.

Mom was a drug user and a prostitute. During the time of the incident, she left her five- and seven-year-old daughters alone in their garden apartment while she scored with her pimp. Before she left, she opened a back window in an attempt to cajole a breeze through the unairconditioned apartment. The girls had pushed a kitchen chair against the window and escaped outside to roam the complex. I imagine this wasn't the first time they had done this. However, on this day, the adventurous older sister scaled the pool's locked fence and fell into the water. She didn't know how to swim.

After the tragic events, the five-year-old was relegated to live with her aunt. Mom was incarcerated for outstanding warrants and faced additional child neglect charges. About a year later, a friend of mine working for the

District Attorney (DA) office informed me that the mom would be reunited with her youngest daughter and that charges were severely lessened.

"They always try to get them back with their parents. It is the best possible outcome for everyone if they are willing to follow their probation," he offered, sensing my frustration. He didn't return my cynicism, but he understood my bias. According to the CDC, more children ages one to four die from drowning than any other cause of death, and for children five to fourteen, drowning is the second leading cause of unintentional death after motor vehicle crashes.[10] I have been blessed with two daughters, and for me, this story adds to the weight of parenting, loving, and caring for my children—and teaching them to swim.

Emma

I'm not a doctor, but my dispatching experiences have placed me in several precarious medical situations. One of my favorites was helping someone deliver their pride and joy. It wasn't a busy day, and I was shooting the breeze with several coworkers in the back pod. I casually answered the phone as an officer approached my station with a stack of documents in his hand for me to notarize. Just another hat I wore for folks in the police department. Prioritizing, I held my finger up to signal to him that I would be a minute.

In the first seconds of the phone call, a very panicked male told me his girlfriend was having a baby! Before I reached for my dust-covered pregnancy and childbirth protocol, I verified that the address was in my jurisdiction. After this quick check, I had responders dispatched in one minute and forty seconds. Two minutes into the call, I was dishing out instructions from my EMD (Emergency Medical Dispatch) protocol prompts.

EMD is a certification that the majority of telecommunicators are required to have based on the services the PSAP offers. Police-only agencies may not require this because they transfer their medical calls, but PSAPs that dispatch for fire and EMS are required to have this certification. With this certification, telecommunicators can quickly triage medical problems, go to the correct protocol, ask pertinent questions, and give very basic medical instructions based on the situation. The protocols and instructions are written by a medical doctor who contracts for the EMD company and then provides them to the PSAPs. Certified EMD telecommunicators can instruct callers to watch the patient very closely until help arrives, control bleeding, turn the patient on their side in case of vomiting, or even administer an EpiPen.

The most complicated protocol cards include instructing CPR and childbirth. CPR happens frequently. Giving childbirth instructions, on the other hand, is a rare telecommunicator experience and a unicorn–bucket list item. I consider myself to be one of the lucky ones who got to have this experience.

The first prompt on the EMD card involved getting the patient to solid ground.

"OK, get her on the floor," I said with surety.

"The baby is almost out!!" he squealed, half excited, half terrified.

"OK sir, I want you to keep her head raised. Let me know when you have this done," I told him.

"I put some pillows under her head, is that OK?" he asked anxiously.

"That's perfect," I encouraged. "Next, I want you to get some dry towels and a blanket to wrap the baby in. Get a string or shoelace to tie around the umbilical cord after delivery. Also get a safety pin if you can." I realized that was an ambitious laundry list. I hoped he would remember it all.

I heard him rushing around. Normally a caller will tune out a dispatcher's instructions, but I think he was hyper-focused with purpose and shock. While he was running around gathering things for his newly formed family, I heard the best sound ever.

"The baby is out!" he screamed with equal parts exhilaration and terror. The cries of a brand-new baby filled the phone.

"OK, you're doing a great job. Keep the baby between the mother's legs and level with her bottom. With one of the towels you gathered, gently wipe off the baby's mouth and nose. Then with the same towel, dry the rest of the baby off as well as you can. Let me know when you are done."

He was breathing heavily into the phone. Panic, elation, and determination were palpable in his silence.

"Alright, I think I did a good job." His first act as a dad was complete.

"Great job! Next take that second clean towel and wrap the baby up, covering the baby's head but not its face. Without pulling the umbilical cord tight, put the baby down between the mother's legs, level with her bottom. Be sure the cord is not wrapped around the baby's neck. The most important thing is to keep the baby and the mother warm." I spouted out a word vomit of really important instructions.

"I can do that," he said with confidence. I smiled knowing this gentleman was amazingly doing everything I said. I could hear the new mom in the background lovingly saying hi to her new baby and whispering how much she loves them. The baby's cries quickly turned into coos. I was not distracted by the love session, although my heart did swell a little. I knew my focus was to provide ample guidance so the responding units would have minimal work to do.

I peeked ahead at my instructions. The card told me to monitor mother and baby for three minutes. I glanced at the clock and the map showcasing my responding units closing in.

"OK sir, are you ready for this next part?" I asked, and he happily agreed.

"We are going to watch the baby closely for three minutes, then tie the cord with that string you got," I read, surprised to have gotten this far before first responders showed up. Either way, I continued. "Without pulling on the cord, tie the string you have tightly around the umbilical cord, about six inches from the baby, but do not cut it. Tie it now, and tell me when it's done," I instructed.

"It's done," he remarked.

"Great! You guys are doing great," I encouraged. From my point of view, his girlfriend was a champ—remaining cool, calm, and collected—and he was holding it together as best he could!

"Do not pull on the cord. The afterbirth or placenta should deliver soon. Tell me if this happens or if anything changes," I said, trying to imagine what I would do in this situation.

"OK, I think it's out," he unconfidently offered.

"OK, if it's out, wrap it in a towel and keep it. The doctor will need to examine it to make sure it all came out," I said with a slight smile, imagining his horror. Hearing more rustling, I could tell he was being a great listener and participating fully.

Soon after this instruction, the fire department arrived on scene and took control of the situation. I glanced at my clock and noticed that nine minutes had passed. What a crazy-fast delivery for that momma. As soon as I hung up the phone, I felt several pairs of eyes were staring at the back of my head. Apparently, when a telecommunicator delivers a baby, it's a stop-everything-and-stare kind of situation. Mouths agape, the first question was if it was a boy or a girl, and I slapped my forehead. I HAD FORGOTTEN TO ASK THE SEX OF THE BABY! *Whoops.* Either way, I set a new center record for the youngest patient, and everyone was happy and healthy—which is all that really mattered.

Lea

During my career, approximately a half dozen shifts have rendered me a comatose mess. After I went home from a graveyard shift one night in March, I knew my number was increasing. A pre-migraine, blurred-vision, nauseated, shoulder-tensed mess. After this night of torrential shit-kicking, our center increased the requirement for minimum staffing during overnight shifts to avoid incredibly stressful incidents like this in the future—a monumental decision that changed the trajectory of staffing in the PSAP.

It began when Amber, a telecommunicator assigned to Channel One, answered an administrative line to help with high call volume. She was speaking with a female who was slurring her words and talking about "cops and how they don't like Black people." She made threats to officers and mentioned having a weapon in her car. My telecommunicator questioned her and asked her name and age, obtaining as much information from her as possible, a difficult task because the female was very uncooperative. After the female hung up, Amber entered an information call for service that highlighted the RP's discontent and threats to law enforcement. Although her location was unknown, documentation was appropriate, and all area personnel were advised.

"Can you believe this chick?" Amber said with her South African accent.

"What's that?" I asked for clarity above the buzz of my own rhythm.

"This nut job on the info call! She's drunk and saying she has a weapon and is gonna kill cops! What is wrong with people?" She finished her distain with her classic Amber catchphrase.

"What is wrong with people, indeed," Alison chimed in.

We continued our banter about the caller's antics. Just another crazy person on the phone. As Amber finished venting, Alison and I dove into answering two 911 calls ringing in simultaneously. We talked to our respective RPs about similar locations and asked matching questions. It was clear within seconds that both our parties were watching the same black sedan weave drunkenly on the interstate. I caught Alison's eye, and we nodded at each other. I covered my microphone and advised her I dropped in the call using mile marker 290. My RP provided a license plate for the vehicle. I added it and then saw Alison's notes appearing in the call narrative. I ran a check on the license plate provided, and surprisingly it was a valid listing to a small black sedan. I knew it was a possible match, so I put the listing in the call notes. Amber aired the information about a possible drunk driver to units in the area. Despite this being in a remote part of our county, a deputy was in very close proximity. Within a minute, he miraculously found the vehicle. He continued to follow safely for several miles, observing driving actions consistent with an intoxicated driver. Despite following the vehicle into the next jurisdiction, he persisted, knowing a potential hazard was on the road; a DUI carried a felony offense in Colorado. Amber scrambled to get him a cover car to initiate a traffic stop, but his remote location made this task more difficult.

Finally, with a cover car on the way, he initiated a traffic stop—the second most dangerous thing an officer can do on shift, next to responding to a domestic violence call. More officer deaths happen with this procedure than any other. As he approached the vehicle, he aired the license plate on Channel One. Not only was it an exact match to the plate my caller had given, but the name on the registration matched the name of the caller Amber had spoken with earlier, the intoxicated female who was threatening deputies and saying she had a weapon.

> "Edward 78 be advised a female matching that name called minutes ago threatening police, claiming to have a weapon," Amber succinctly relayed the pertinent information.

> "Edward 78 I copy. Vehicle is occupied one time [with one occupant]. I will wait to approach with cover," he said with a flutter in his voice.

> "Channel One is on emergency for Edward 78," Amber immediately decided after putting the pieces together and assessing the danger.

"Edward 81 I am enroute Code 3," cover aired over the blast of his sirens.

At this moment, it was very clear that everything had happened for a reason. There was a reason Amber, who normally would not answer the phone while assigned to Channel One, had picked up the admin line to talk to this lady and had committed her name to memory. Goosebumps peppered my skin.

Amber, Alison, and I waited to see how the events of the traffic stop would transpire. I turned Amber's radio up on my console so I could keep tabs on what was going on, despite the deluge of emergency calls I continued to triage.

"Edward 78 there is an assault rifle in the car. Shots fired," he aired, changing the trajectory of this call. "She also is refusing to come out," he added.

"Copy at 0236," Amber timestamped.

"Edward 81 I am two minutes out," cover confirmed.

After this action upped the ante, five area agencies blared to assist on the traffic stop. I paged the SWAT team for assistance with a barricaded subject. My command staff also requested that we call the bearcat, a heavily armored vehicle that adds protection to first responders in hostile situations. Additionally, due to the nature of this event, the CIRT needed to be dispatched to investigate if the first responder's use of force was warranted. All these notifications amounted to complete chaos. My teammates and I struggled to keep up with the deluge. Amber was yelling out her requests for help, while Alison, the overwhelmed Channel Two telecommunicator, attempted to handle radio traffic for the rest of the county. I alone manned the phones, monitored MetroNet, paged secondary responders, and worked with command staff to make decisions based on our staffing in the center. We were all busy. In the middle of all of this, being the acting supervisor, I knew Alison needed a ten-minute break to pump. Although I hadn't yet experienced the ache of a full breast myself, a small kick inside my belly reminded me my time was coming.

"Alison, if you don't go now, I don't know that you will get a chance," I said, seizing a small window of opportunity.

"Are you sure?" she asked skeptically.

"Now or never, girl." I affirmed, clicking into Channel Two.

She pulled her headset off and hustled toward the breakroom. Eleven long minutes later she returned to three 911 calls, two admin lines on hold, a warrant confirmation repeatedly dinging in our terminal inbox, and two telecommunicators with their hair on fire.

Although Alison had returned to help with the workload, our sinking ship continued to take on serious water. Amber was still assisting with the emergency call on Channel One and the rest of the county was going up in flames as two Priority One calls—an assault in progress and a burglary—needed to be dispatched. The universe was hell-bent on not giving us a break! We got our asses handed to us for the next three hours, but we emerged on the other side with no injured citizens or deputies.

Eventually, multiple members of two jurisdictions' SWAT teams forced the disgruntled and intoxicated female out of her car, and she was mad as a hornet. She went kicking and screaming to the hospital, where she was medically sedated by emergency room personnel. After she was medically cleared, she was transported to the jail and booked for warrants and other new charges. What was worse, the CIRT team found a vacuum cleaner attachment in her car that she had been brandishing, not an assault rifle.

Considering our current climate, I'm grateful that no one got hurt; that outcome is becoming increasingly rare in policing incidents. Even so, that night gave me the worst migraine I have ever had. My migraine, tension, and pain lasted all weekend. My legacy of this night lives on, not as an epic headache, but because of the resulting PSAP staffing changes. After the effects of this shift, I voiced my concerns about the dangerously low staffing levels and the undue pressure put on the room. Leadership was open to my feedback and mandated a higher minimum staffing requirement for graveyard shift. That was a drumbeat I happily marched to and benefitted from on my future years working the overnight shift.

Lea

One of my all-time favorite movies is *Notting Hill*. I love the story, the subtle humor, Hugh Grant, and of course the famous line, "I am just a girl, standing in front of a boy, asking him to love her." The hopeless romantic inside me melts every time. The unsung hero in this classic treasure is the perpetually high, misfit roommate, Spike. In one scene he bursts into the flat and announces, "Just going to the kitchen to get some food, then I'm going to tell you a story that will make your balls shrink to the size of raisins. . ."[11]

In my humble opinion, this classic line rivals the one about boys and girls loving each other, and I have used this line to predicate many crazy stories. Kind of like an exclamation point appetizer. Well, folks, I have a story that will make your balls shrink to the size of raisins.

I was working another graveyard Christmas Eve shift. My heart was full after fabulous family time spent eating delicious food and watching my baby, now a demonstrative three-year-old, tear gleefully through mounds of gifts while my one-year-old smiled and snuggled with her grandpa. This year Santa creatively came down the chimney during nap time to accommodate my shift. So nice of Santa to make a special run for my girls. When I reported for duty later that night, everyone in the center shared the same festive mood. I opted to work Channel One and, feeling the Christmas spirit, I aired a Christmas message at midnight. For several minutes afterward, deputies chimed in with heartfelt "Merry Christmas" choruses and general goodwill. The cheer was palpable in their voices as if we were sitting around sipping hot toddies in front of the fire watching a beloved movie. We almost forgot that we were all sitting at work and not home with family. Almost.

Twenty-five minutes into Christmas, I heard my call taker on a 911 line from across the room. Anticipating a call for service, I refreshed my CAD queue and saw the call for service appear, an accident with unknown injuries on a major highway—one of the two major US highways we patrol. In this part of the county, the roads are dark, sinuous, and very disorienting to those who are passing through. Accidents in this area can be very destructive because of the high speeds and noncompliance to seatbelt and DUI laws. Our warm and fuzzy Christmas came to an abrupt halt with my call taker's first line of narrative: "RP is a trucker. Thinks he hit a body."

What the heck, I whispered under my breath. *This cannot be real.* The next line read, "Initially said human body but not sure if deer." *Phew! Still sad, but a deer was better than a human body*, I thought, prioritizing my holy trinity. I aired the information and assigned a deputy to the call. After I finished, an unknown voice piped up with his badge number on the radio. Radio protocol dictates that when a unit isn't signed into the CAD but needs to initiate a radio transmission, a badge number can be used instead of a callsign.

"Star 18097, go ahead..." I answered, echoing his identifier.

"I just ran over it, too, in my personal vehicle. I think it was a deer," he noted succinctly.

As this information was aired, a third 911 caller hit the object, and the female RP resolutely declared that it was a human body. Keeping a count, that was two for a body and one for a deer. I winced, knowing either way this call would be gruesome. The original truck driver RP had pulled over to inspect his load and now reported that the accident had punctured his gas line, causing an additional hazard on the highway. All this information culminated in a lights and sirens response from my responding units.

"Star 18097," he flagged me again for a transmission.

"Go ahead," I acquiesced, not really wanting his update.

"After getting closer, this is a human body. DOA." The shoe dropped. Everyone in the room gasped. "The highway needs to be shut down. It's all over the eastbound lanes of traffic." *Gross.*

All remaining holiday cheer was instantly sucked from the room. Two of my partners started calling neighboring agencies for emergency help to shut down the highway.

As the call progressed, I ran a couple of plates for the deputies, updated rescue about the situation, and maintained communication on MetroNet to the responding neighboring agencies. Units on scene quickly determined that the body came from a different vehicle on the highway involved in a single-vehicle rollover crash. Witnesses reported the vehicle driving in the westbound lanes at excessive speeds just before the truck driver phoned about hitting the body. Deputies ascertained by the smell in the air and the empty bottles in the car that this person was extremely intoxicated. They also surmised that the driver lost control of the vehicle and, not wearing a seatbelt, was ejected into the eastbound lane of traffic where multiple cars ran over the body, spreading debris one hundred yards down the highway.

According to my responding sergeant, who has over twenty-one years of experience, it was one of the most gruesome things he had ever witnessed. After he cleared the scene, he called in. I asked him all the questions I could think of. (Please move forward to the next chapter if you are not prepared for some horrific Sweeney Todd details.)

"What the heck happened?" I began. To this initial question, he described the above details, plus the single shoe with a severed leg still attached on the side of the road. Investigators presumed this was where the subject landed after the ejection and before he was hit, dismembered, and dragged the length of a football field. *Yuck.*

"Did you all find the head? What body parts are we talking about here?" I asked, revealing my dark side.

"No, Lea," he chuckled. "Not yet." He continued, telling me they found the torso, but they wouldn't know for sure until the coroner responded. No arms either. He suspected a coyote would probably have a wonderful Christmas dinner.

"How many cars hit him?" I asked next, eager to hear the gory details. He estimated five to seven, looking at the bloody tire marks. Of course, the semi did the worst damage. I contemplated his answer and quickly calculated how many 911 calls we had received. Only four drivers reported a run-in with the body; knowing this, I suspected there were more drunk drivers on the road who hadn't reported what they had witnessed. Just the week before, I had been talking to a deputy who estimated that on a weekend or a holiday if he pulls over eight cars, he will get one DUI. (Those odds are outrageous considering all the services available now for rides. Please, don't drink and drive!)

"What punctured the gas line?" I asked next. He was uncertain but suspected the spine.

"Do you think he was dead before he got hit by the first car?" I questioned.

"I sure hope so, for his sake! Not that he deserves what happened. Drunk driving without a seatbelt tends to be a user-corrected problem. At least he didn't take anyone else down with him," he said.

"How do you know he was drunk? Is there any way to tell?" I asked out of curiosity. He described the smell that assaulted his nostrils the moment he opened his patrol car door. I silently wondered how drunk you must be for the stench of alcohol to thoroughly permeate the scene where your blood and guts are strewn over one hundred yards. I can only hope and pray this poor bastard didn't feel pain.

"How are you going to clean that up? What is the coroner going to do?" I asked, pondering the logistics.

"Unfortunately, the fire department and the coroner have their work cut out for them." He added that they would have to comb the scene and collect the body part, a task made all the more difficult because of the nighttime darkness. After this was complete, the fire department would use their high-pressure hoses to wash the surface of the highway.

"Is everyone on scene OK?" I switched gears. The answer was a resounding yes, but everyone agreed this was the worst and most horrendous scene they had ever encountered.

"Anything else you want to tell me?" I asked like a counselor.

"I'm pretty sure I saw an optic nerve on the side of the road. It looked like a snake on the curb! It wasn't attached to an eyeball, but it was definitely an optic nerve." *Wow.*

Are we at raisins yet?

Lea

One of the most epic scenes in the *Lord of the Rings* trilogy is when Gandalf stands before the demon in the Mines of Moria and declares that the enemy shall not pass. With a gesture of power and strength, Gandalf raises his staff and strikes the stone bridge below him. The bridge crumbles, and with it falls not only the enemy but Gandalf himself. Whenever I think of this next story, I envision this epic scene. Just like Gandalf, the employee gate heroically stopped evil one warm summer night. Despite being broken half the time and always needing maintenance, it did its job that night and prevented something sinister from gaining access to all of us. I shudder imagining the scenario if the gate had remained open, as it often did.

In the wee hours of that morning, deputies and officers had unofficially stopped initiating calls in order to write their reports and catch up on their administrative duties. My coworkers and I used this lull to binge a few more episodes in a series. Probably something silly like *Vampire Diaries* or *You*.

Interrupting our binging progress, one of our favorite deputies called with a suspicious vehicle at the employee entrance. Jordan, operating Channel One, dutifully documented the call and assigned the cover car. We all thought nothing of it and resumed our trash TV. Five minutes passed, and a status check resulted in a C4 response; everything was fine.

And then. . .

"Frank 41 SHOTS FIRED!" he called, out of breath.

"Channel One is on emergency at 0421," Jordan responded.

Whoa! That escalated quickly. The moment froze as I heard this over the radio. That same voice was just up in the PSAP discussing the latest round of baby names he thought up for my unborn child. We laughed like we always did when he visited. When I first met him, he was a recruit assigned to shadow me for a few hours. Fast friends, we swapped origin stories and I tested his claim of fluency in Arabic. His screams jolted me to the present, my body tensing, and everything becoming both sharp and distant as adrenaline pumped through my veins. My brain was trying to process my first officer-involved shooting; my mouth was full of cotton and my hands were suddenly encased in molasses. Every keystroke required Herculean effort. Despite not being on the radio, I knew I needed to support Jordan in whatever way she needed so that she could champion the voices on scene.

Within seconds, our world erupted. Everyone in the county who heard the transmission was racing over to help. A deputy, who was inside the gate preparing to go back to the road after a meal break, abandoned his car to jump the eight-foot fence and help deputies on the other side. (Thank goodness he was six-foot-seven-inches and kind of a beast.) After this incident a pedestrian gate was installed so no deputy would ever have to scale the gate again.

Soon the scene was crawling with deputies and officers from neighboring agencies, and the incident finished in a matter of minutes. Afterward, we learned the tragic tale of what had transpired. An ex-jail employee had received a dishonorable dismissal from his duties, and there was some lingering tension. Following his termination, his life took a darker path, and his exasperated mental health issues led to severe substance abuse. A recipe for disaster. In a moment of despair, he drove to the station, parked in front of the gate by the badge reader, and put a loaded gun on his lap while he waited. And waited. And waited.

It didn't take long for a deputy to pull behind him at the gate. When the car didn't move, the deputy initiated the first radio transmission about the suspicious vehicle. He attempted to contact the driver and, based on the immediate red flags, asked for a cover car. This deputy was a smooth talker. Ex-military. Smart. Relatable. Also armed with a CIT (Critical Incident Training) certification, which indicates specialized training in de-escalation tactics and mental health episodes. The universe couldn't have sent a more perfect candidate to talk to this lone wolf! Cover arrived, and the team attempted to talk, negotiate, and de-escalate the situation. During this negotiation, a status check was performed, and things were simmering but not boiling red hot—yet.

A switch flipped. The subject made threatening statements and lifted the gun off his lap with his hand on the trigger. Neither of my units hesitated.

They both shot this man. Kill or be killed. After shooting him, they promptly pulled him out of the car to administer CPR and try to save his life. Rescue arrived two minutes later and pronounced him dead on arrival.

After this incident, all directly involved parties were put on administrative leave pending the outcome of the internal affairs investigation. This is a standard practice for all agencies to determine if the use of force was appropriate. However, IA investigations are very difficult mentally, emotionally, and physically for the officers involved. I know the deputies who pulled their triggers that night did not do so lightly. They were in danger, and they acted on it. The investigation, which lasted a little more than a month, cleared them both, but I saw the resulting invisible scars on each of their souls. To make that terrible choice is nothing short of torture. Throughout my career, I witnessed so many deputies after instances like this—their eyes sunken and hollow from lack of sleep, their hygiene lax from the stress, their faces ashen and dark from unhealthy coping skills.

This incident, my first officer-involved shooting, affected me profoundly. I was eternally grateful that my deputies were not hurt. I had experienced close calls and crazy incidents of violence involving other team members, but this time, my *friend* was out there. Someone I cared about. It changed my perspective and made me an agency advocate for mental health and peer-to-peer support. I also stopped cursing the gate every time it malfunctioned because I knew that when I needed it most, it would rise or remain closed as it should. To protect and serve.

Fate(al)

Emma

911 telecommunicators hear the worst of the worst. Research has now acknowledged that telecommunicators can suffer PTSD simply from the horrible sounds heard on the job. I applaud mental health professionals who acknowledge trauma can occur in the absence of physical presence or sight. I also have hope that with more research and resources aligned with this type of PTSD, further treatment for the *first*–first responders can be the new norm.

It's a very surreal experience when all you hear are words, and your brain paints the most vivid pictures with excruciating detail in order to complete thoughts and fully process what is being heard. Occasionally, I wished this mechanism did not work because these pictures are not always accurate depictions of reality. However, emergency telecommunicators cannot correct the pictures because they never see the outcome; instead, horrifying mental images and sounds create a PTSD loop that never closes.

I felt the very real effects of PTSD during a perfect storm of fateful circumstances aligning with a tragic accident. As a supervisor, I don't always answer phones or monitor a radio channel. My responsibilities usually include admin tasks, call audits, and supporting my team as they need. On this particular day, someone had called in sick, so I came in early for my shift to help. I was answering calls to meet minimum staffing during the busiest part of the day. I had one of the best crews! Top-notch telecommunicators. However, even on the busiest day with the worst calls, being short-staffed can be nothing less than an ass-kicking. This day was that day.

As we've described earlier, cellular calls get routed to PSAPs based on geography and cell tower location. A 911 call from a cell phone bounces off cell towers that are in the area and support the phone carrier (which is why it pays to have good service) and directs the phone call to the closest PSAP. When you don't have good cell service or you're on a cheap basic plan, then the call tries to connect to a tower that supports the cell carrier. This results in 911 phone calls occasionally being routed to the wrong PSAP. But sometimes fate intervenes.

"911, what is the address of the emergency?" I answered the incoming line dutifully. But all I could hear on the other end of the phone was garbled speech. I knew they had horrible reception.

"Hello, can you hear me?" I tried again. In the moments after this and through bad reception, I deciphered something about a rollover accident on I-25. Using my locating resources (thank goodness we have these), I was able to verify that the phone was calling from somewhere on I-25, the large north–south interstate that cuts Colorado in half.

Trusting my gut, I entered an injury accident per protocol at the guestimate location I saw on my map.

Then the call disconnected, and I was left with a dial tone buzzing loudly in my ear. Based on the location of the accident shown on my map, I absolutely could have punted this call to a different agency for follow-up, but at that moment I chose otherwise. I thought, *if I didn't get a location verification from the caller and they don't have service, what are the chances that another agency will get good information?* Slim. It would just be confusing, so I decided to keep the call and not punt to another PSAP. Following protocol, I called the number back.

"Hey, this is 911. We just got a call from this number. Can you hear me?" I asked.

Thanks to a greatly improved phone connection, the conversation started flowing. Continuing to follow my gut, I chose to stay on the line instead of transferring the caller to another agency. My PSAP was sending fire and rescue resources to the accident, so I maintained control of the call.

The initial male who called in was now describing a single vehicle rollover, multiple ejections, and at least one child dead. After rambling all this off through his shock, he then handed the phone to a female, who was coincidently an off-duty paramedic.

The events that followed are burned into my brain. The off-duty paramedic started brilliantly triaging every patient by herself while talking to me on speakerphone. She relayed vital details as I typed ferociously to get all those details to responding firefighters and paramedics. I quickly realized that she did not need the very basic medical instructions that I was certified to give. My role was clearly a dutiful note-taker.

One by one she lined up her patients. There was a male with an obvious broken leg and broken back. Another was a female, Code Black—a term used to qualify a patient with the status DOA (dead on arrival). Another Code Black was a baby, ejected into the field. A second baby—a twin—wasn't conscious or breathing when she started triaging. A third child was severely injured. The paramedic quickly turned her attention to the baby who wasn't breathing. I listened as she masterfully talked her way through intubating the baby on the side of the road. The glorious, gut-wrenching sound of a baby gasping for air made my heart soar. The baby quickly transitioned from not breathing to a somewhat stable condition because of the efforts of this angel RP. Soon after, this infant was flown via Flight for Life to Children's Hospital. I typed everything she said word for word. Her notes were not hopeful, but her meticulous attention to detail prepared first responders for the mass casualty event.

The sounds I heard painted such a vivid picture in my brain. Thuds as she moved bodies around. Crying, pain, chaos, vehicle wreckage, and devastation. My imagination could picture the scene, but I could not see faces, a haunting memory that does not disappear.

I waited on the phone with her—we were two kindred souls fighting for life and desperately waiting for the fire department. When units arrived, I started listening to the radio traffic.

I'm not an emotional person, but that call rocked me to my core. I looked at one of my partners, and she knew I needed to take a break, regardless of how short-staffed we were. Thirty seconds of crying in the bathroom was all I could afford. My team needed me back on the floor, so I left my tears in the bathroom and finished my twelve-hour shift.

A week later I attended a debriefing with therapy dogs. For confidentiality reasons, I can't go into detail about what happened in that room, but I left knowing we did everything we could. I learned details that helped complete the picture my mind had already painted. This was a family not wearing seatbelts, driving down the road, who lost control. The mom died instantly, and the father lived and sustained back injuries and a broken femur. One of the twins died immediately after being ejected from the vehicle, while the other twin succumbed to her injuries after being treated at a local hospital. The other toddler in the car lived but suffered severe brain injuries.

Please buckle up. Seatbelts save lives.

This incident's unfolding was nothing but fate—or perhaps divine intervention. Everything clicked the way it was supposed to that day. I instinctually kept the phone call and took diligent notes. The RP was an off-duty paramedic who delivered perfect updates and helped prepare the fire department. Her updates also assisted my team's decision to call for helicopters early instead of waiting. All the calls for assistance were made correctly and relayed important updates without error. The communication between departments was flawless. Nothing could have been better.

I have been asked many times how I can be OK with people dying and sad outcomes. First and foremost, I know my Lord and Savior only brings His children home when it is their time. Second, I'm very desensitized to the horrors of this job because of my tenure. However, in situations like these when it doesn't always make sense, I know that everything happens for a reason, which I know is so cliché but also true. In this situation, everything clicked and gave those kids and that dad the best chance for survival! This is the most painful reality a 911 telecommunicator faces: sometimes doing the absolute best job possible still results in failure.

Lea

The running joke with my husband every time I left for work included a standard salutation before I kissed him and jutted out the door. "Well, it's time for me to go save lives!" I would say with gusto—or disdain, depending on how the week was going and how much sleep I had gotten. The truth is when I was growing up, I had no idea what I wanted to do with my life. In college I bounced between a couple of majors and several jobs. Then I tripped into a paid teaching associate gig that came with a master's degree. After conquering that hill I thought, *what now*? Reevaluating and assessing my muddled work history, which included everything from lifeguarding to ad sales and marketing, I was left puzzled. Sydney Bristow's sidekick wasn't an option, despite my years watching *Alias* and fantasizing about jumping out of an airplane before gracefully touching down in my lightweight parachute and kick-ass heels to a Tuscan villa glamazon party. A groovy Smash Mouth tune plays in the background as I grab a flute of champagne, acting like nothing happened while I search the party guests to find my contact and complete a top-secret spy mission. This was my fantasy.

In reality, the only ticking time bomb in my life was two toddlers screaming and melting down if I didn't have dinner ready by five o'clock. No wires to cut. No heated countdowns. No heels. No makeup. No fun wigs. No crazy cool language skills. No gadgets from Marshall. No new stamp on my passport every week. Just a working mom running on four hours of sleep, the graveyard shift special. Despite all the stuff I didn't have in common with my heroine, we did share some commonalities. Sydney Bristow worked diligently, and no one saw the good work she did. Similar to this was the role I played as a *first*–first responder—no credit, kudos, or attention awaited after the long and suffering shifts. My workflow included taking the call, sending the help, and most of the time never knowing the outcome.

Throughout the series, Sydney wonders if her double life ever mattered. I often felt the same. Reflecting now, I can say with absolute clarity that my time wearing the headset made an amazing difference. I smirk now thinking about the joke shared with my husband about leaving to save lives. Unspoken between us, we both knew it wasn't a joke.

Many calls changed people's lives. I was the calm voice that initiated rescue's response to the jail deputy's panicked 911 call for an inmate who attempted suicide. The inmate lived. Another time, I coordinated police and rescue response after a daughter shot her mother. The deputy who responded was an ex-army medic who arrived on scene and triaged the wound so well that the mother not only lived but also didn't lose her arm! Moreover, I have helped support the efforts of first responders pulling people from burning buildings and smashed vehicles. Remembering some of these moments that occurred as my cold food taunted me and I battled sleeplessness, I can now clearly see through the muck and mire to the brighter side. The silver lining. The rainbow.

One of the most potent rainbow stories begins with a family that drove through our metro area and decided to stop for the night. The family, including thirteen-year-old twin girls, had lived in northern Colorado for five years, incurring a lot of hardship when COVID-19 shut down the world. They, like many others, decided to move to be closer to family, packing up their lives and heading south. Their clothes, birth certificates, and even their daughter's wheelchair were included in their epic haul. As they laid their heads for some much-needed rest, pure evil broke into the family's truck and stole the truck and everything beloved inside. Everything they owned. Gone.

After our PSAP received the call and responding deputies took the crime report, the story garnered attention from many within the agency and eventually snowballed into massive news coverage. Initially, the Fraternal Order of Police (FOP) lodge spread the word of the auto theft, and police union members donated money. Not long after that, another deputy donated a wheelchair he had lying around his house. I eventually caught wind of the story around the water cooler and donated clothes and other household items. Soon enough, the news picked up the story and made waves in the community. A call went out for necessary items. The family was blessed with enough money to buy a new vehicle and recoup their losses. They were also blessed with enough items to start the brand-new life they desired. Thanks be to God!

A similar rainbow story began with a gas station robbery at four o'clock in the morning. A fourteen-year-old walked into his local gas station and pulled a gun on the clerk, demanding money. The teen was face-to-face with a fifty-seven-year-old gas station graveyard attendant who had clerked this register for eighteen years. In response to the threat, he pulled out his own legal concealed carry weapon. (For the record, if a gun is forced into your face and money or possessions are demanded, just give it up. Do not be a hero; your life is worth more.) In this situation, however, shots were fired from both guns, and the fourteen-year-old was injured in the exchange. The clerk called 911, and while my partner triaged the call, I dispatched deputies. In the end, the robber was transported to the hospital where he was successfully treated for his wounds. And the gas station attendant was fired.

Many of our deputies had been going to that gas station for refuge for years. It was a well-known, safe location to grab a coffee and write a report. The clerk was loved by many at the agency, so his shocking termination sent waves through the sheriff's office. And I have learned this from our tight-knit family: when something strikes a chord, *it sings*. Soon employees started a fund for this attendant. I didn't know him personally, but you better believe I put in money to help him. This man was brave (or stupid) enough to stare down the barrel of a gun and protect himself! That gumption, coupled with the fact that he had personally shepherded many at the agency, earned a couple of bucks from me. The fund was very successful, and I can only hope it helped this brave man start a new career for himself.

Not all superheroes wear capes. They also don't have to wear fancy wigs, lipstick, or boots and be armed with a USB drive. Some of them wear uniforms, badges, radios, guns, or headsets. My job often entailed being on the line with callers during the worst three minutes of their lives. However, in that horror and terror, opportunities for giving, supporting, and loving the community were born. These cases truly display our truest calling: to help others on this earth!

Lea

Anyone who has watched *Jackass* or *Dude Perfect* knows how crazy young men can be. Call it their underdeveloped brain and inflated sense of self. Call it a larger-than-life attitude. Call it an expected hike in an insurance policy. Call it whatever you want, but it is a very real phenomenon.

In my career, I have talked to many young males who made bad decisions. But nothing takes the cake like a call that involved a young man trying to stop his mom's truck from being stolen. Great heart, bad actions! Around five in the morning (this is a popular time for the pot to be stirred), my teammates and I were enjoying a friendly game of cards. It had been snowing during the entire shift, and we lamented having to soon scrape our cars and drive home on the icy roads. Before we could contemplate too much, four 911s simultaneously pierced our conversation. After exchanging befuddled looks, we scattered to our stations and dove into action.

My partner and I both answered calls from supporting actors in the unfolding tale. We quickly typed and dutifully obtained the necessary information to get the call in for service as soon as possible. Auto theft had just occurred. Listening across the room, I could hear that the calls in triage were the same event. My caller, a maintenance man shoveling snow in the hotel parking lot, witnessed a truck being stolen. I dropped my call in for service first and heard the speedy dispatch on Channel One. Being a Priority One call, it had to go out quickly. As the call progressed, two different telecommunicators wove a narrative from two different witnesses reporting the same crime. A similar story rang out about a vehicle being stolen in very cold weather. Soon my caller could no longer see the truck, and I disconnected the call, knowing he could not provide further information.

Just then two other 911 calls rang out. My partners gobbled up both before I could click on either line. I read both notes; Jaime was talking with the son of the truck owner. He had seen the truck being stolen and decided to jump in the pickup bed as it was driving off. Smooth and very stupid move. After he jumped into the truck, his mom got in her vehicle to follow the stolen truck with her son stowed in the truck bed. She also called 911 and was reporting the same incident from her point of view to my other teammate, Maggie. What started as a chaotic 911 flurry was now a full-fledged family affair. I was sure the next call would be from a second cousin!

The son in the truck bed wore only a T-shirt as the thieves attempted to navigate the icy and snowy roads. Soon he was talking with us through chattering teeth. I pictured an epic Titanic-esque scene where steamy breath escaped his lips, and the frosted tips of his hair crowned his face as he rolled around aimlessly in the back of the pickup.

Fortuitously deputies were already in the area, and they joined the call, located the caravan, and started a pursuit within minutes.

I use the word *pursuit* lightly. Speeds were called out at 30 mph as everyone traversed the dangerous roads. Thanks to the radio, cover was in position ahead with tire-puncturing tools deployed in the roadway. Knowing this, my units backed off the truck. Everyone rolled through the intersection, and nothing happened. Mom, following too closely in her personal vehicle, didn't get the message about backing off the truck, so the units pulled the Stop Sticks, the large rolls with nails that first responders use to flatten tires during pursuits, in consideration of her safety. *Jeez.*

Speeds crested 45 mph; the pursuit was still very much alive. As they passed through other police jurisdictions, we asked for additional assistance. Like lighting beacons between Gondor and Rohan, we all made calls for aid. All attempts were shot down. Apparently, it was a hot night for auto thefts—multiple cars had been taken from a Ferrari dealership. I rolled my eyes, disconnecting my call and extinguishing my lantern of hope for help.

The truck turned northbound on a major artery that ran through multiple jurisdictions. I started to light the fires of all the jurisdictions in that direction, desperately looking for another agency to assist us. I checked in with Jaime, on the phone with the SYM in the bed of the truck, and she worriedly advised she could hear him shivering now.

All the north jurisdictions advised they copied the call, but they were not allowed to engage in the pursuit for undisclosed policy reasons. King Theoden's character in *The Lord of the Rings* echoed in my mind, "Where was Gondor when the Westfold fell? Where was Gondor when our enemies

closed in around us!? Where was Gon—No, my Lord Aragorn, we are alone."
[12]

We were alone. An administrative phone call pierced the chaos—my dayshift lieutenant, who brought with him fifteen years of road experience! Finally, I breathed. Up until this moment, the highest-ranking commander on shift was a newly promoted sergeant. She had been performing well, but this complex call required more expertise than she had under her belt. The radio traffic was as messy as the roads, and the inexperience of a green graveyard team was showing. But nobody had died yet, so I'd say we were breaking even.

"Why are we following this stolen vehicle?" my dayshift lieutenant asked kindly, a hint of sarcasm in his voice.

"Well, sir, there is a civilian in the bed of the truck. He jumped in while it was being stolen," I informed him.

"Oh, well that was dumb," he said dryly.

"I know, sir," I replied.

"OK, and we are still talking to him, right?" he confirmed.

"Yes."

"Well, tell him to jump out!" he said matter-of-factly.

"Um, OK? I know the speeds are low, but you really want us to do that?" I asked. Normally we don't advise that on 911. Recorded lines, lawsuits, and all.

"Hell yeah! Then we can stop chasing, which is a much more dangerous situation," he said with confidence.

"OK, we will give it a shot!" I said, bolstered by his confidence. I turned to Jaime and told her the new plan. Armed with this information, the SYM considered his options. Would he have enough gumption to do it?

Meanwhile, my sergeant and several other deputies set up a Stop Stick reprise a couple of intersections north. As the truck approached the intersection, everything happened quickly and harmoniously. The thieves driving the truck saw all the cop cars and slowed down. Feeling the speeds ease up, the SYM took his chance for liberty and jumped from the bed of the truck. He landed on the ground and ran to the sidewalk, uninjured. As the truck bed released his weight, the driver struggled on the ice, plowing straight into the Stop Sticks. Disabled. In a last-ditch effort, the driver attempted to flee on foot, but instead landed in the arms of deputies. The SYM, still speaking to us on an emergency line, gave a play-by-play of the scene: restraint efforts, a lot of shouting, a gun falling out of the suspect's pants, then deputies tasing the suspect to properly detain him. Another occupant, still in the truck, complied with all commands and was detained without incident.

Well, hot dang! All that activity took us right up to six o'clock in the morning. Adrenaline rush be damned, I was ready for my bed after that amazing effort. It all came together beautifully, and no one was hurt. I am glad, at least in the case of SYM, that I have only daughters.

Lea

One of my favorite communication theories that I studied while getting my master's degree was the symbolic convergence theory. This theory suggests that experiences, especially those shared in fantasy, bind members of a group together. *Fantasy* is interpreted as setting, characters, and action—the masterful combining of these literary components powerfully draws folks together! Think *Harry Potter, Lord of the Rings,* or *Big Bang Theory.* Any story that creates a connection between people gives this theory credence. Telecommunicators share a lot of stories. Every call represented a fantasy with a new cast, plot, and setting. Every call presented an opportunity to connect the room. Some calls accomplished this more than others. Dillon was definitely one of those calls. His sordid tale, causing us so much hardship one night, became a regular joke around the proverbial water cooler, especially during the winter months. Will you join me in our convergence?

Setting

Colorado is known for some serious winter weather. Natives often share their favorite memories about the crazy weather.

"Remember the blizzard of '03?" is a typical winter weather conversation starter as the snow starts to fall. That was the year my sisters and I bundled up and took turns jumping fifteen feet off our deck into huge snow drifts below.

More recently in March 2019, Colorado had its first "bomb cyclone," a winter version of a hurricane. And it was. This storm was epic. Incredibly windy. Bone-chilling cold. Snow blowing everywhere. The entire state closed! I dutifully reported for my shift to help those who risked their lives and the lives of others by carelessly venturing out into the storm—like the mom who casually loaded up her kids to go to the store then got stuck in a snow drift; my deputy was consequently stuck attempting to respond to her location. Thankfully their full tanks of gas kept both vehicles heated throughout the night. So many similar stories occurred during that storm.

The night Dillon called had serious bomb cyclone vibes as I was, again, working graveyards during a full-force winter storm. The temperatures dipped below zero, which is rare for Colorado. *Colder than a well-digger's ass*, as a coworker always said. My teammates and I were playing cards between busy spells of activity. Soon a 911 call rang out, disturbing our competitive game of Hand and Foot. I trudged over to my console in my snow boots to answer. My ear was greeted by a panicked female on the line. After I cajoled her to take a few deep breaths and give me her name, I started my questioning.

Characters & Action

I quickly deduced that the female was calling from a motel along the highway in the remote part of our county. She was safe and warm, but her partner was not. Earlier when their car broke down, she called for help, seeing no other way to get out of the storm. After she called the state patrol, her partner decided to leave under the pretense of looking for help. In reality, he had outstanding warrants and feared a confrontation with police would garner him a night in the slammer.

She prioritized her life and the child they were traveling with and decided to stay put. A state trooper showed up and called for a tow truck, then transported her and her child to the motel for the night. When she got to the motel, she called her partner. He told her he was out in the storm, lost and freezing. She then called 911 again and got me. She pleaded with us to locate her partner and give him a ride. She mentioned he had out-of-state warrants, but didn't want him to get hurt.

I asked for his location. She didn't know. I then instructed her to message him and tell him to call 911 so I could work off the location information from his phone. She acquiesced, and thirty seconds later another 911 rang in. I knew it had to be him. I disconnected with the female and clicked into the new line.

"911, where is your emergency?" I asked.

"I don't know," he said plainly.

"Are you out in the cold? I think I just spoke to your friend. She is worried about you," I said to provide him the context.

"Yeah, I am cold. I don't know where I am though." He had a gruff voice that trembled, no doubt because of the frigid temperature. While we talked,

I worked with my mapping and location software to attempt to pinpoint his location. Instantly I received some cross streets. He was walking along the road in a very remote area, so I updated the call location to reflect all this information.

"Do you want us to send someone to help you?" I offered.

"Um, I am not sure. I just want to get to the motel," he answered slyly, clearly wanting to avoid the deputies.

"What is your name?"

"Dillon."

"OK, Dillon. What is your last name and birthdate?" He provided the information freely. This was not routine questioning for callers, but knowing he had potential warrants, I wanted to dig deeper and find his dirty laundry. As I ran his name in the system, the line disconnected. Either he terminated the call because he knew what I was up to, or it happened because of bad service. As soon as I read his warrant results, I realized it was probably because of the former. Dillon, my chilly new friend, was the proud owner of a felony warrant for burglary in Missouri with a no-bond hold. Full extradition. His warrant was also flagged for violent tendencies. This was a major warrant for a very serious crime.

I dictated that information in the call, and Mallory updated the responding deputies. At this point, a sergeant piped up on Channel One and asked us to send a neighboring agency to assist due to the slow response time and the warrant.

Soon a 911 call rang in again. Dillon's number.

"Dillon, I see you have a warrant out of Missouri. If we come to help you, are you going to be compliant with our deputies?" I asked, not mincing words.

"Well, are they going to bring me to the motel?" he deadpanned. *No. They will bring you to jail.*

"I don't know what they are going to do. Right now, I have them on the way to help you because you are cold and in the storm," I said, trying to sell the goodwill effort.

"I am c-c-cold," he stuttered.

"Do you want us to help you?" I asked again for his buy-in.

"Yeah!" he replied, reflecting on his dire condition. I checked the temperatures. It was 6 degrees below zero outside, not including the wind chill. By my estimates, he had been out there for six hours. Hypothermia can set in with minimal exposure to the elements at 32 degrees Fahrenheit. I was concerned for Dillon in this situation.

"I do have help on the way. Any idea of where you are now? See any cross streets?" I tried to get a better location to narrow down the needle in a haystack my deputies were going to hunt.

"N-nnn-ooo," he shivered.

"OK, I am working off the location I have from your cell phone. It is not always accurate, but I have help on the way. You need to keep moving, though. If you stop your body will start getting really cold," I instructed.

The line disconnected. I attempted to call him back. No answer.

Just then my acting lieutenant started asking me direct questions about the situation on Channel Two, which I had been working all night. I summarized what I knew about the current situation and that the subject was no longer calling or picking up his phone. With that information, the lieutenant requested a phone ping.

I made the call to the cell phone provider and asked for a phone ping. In this situation, we had enough to get a ping because Dillon had called 911 and there was a threat to his life because of the winter storm. Pings always took an exorbitant amount of time because telecommunicators have to verify that the caller called 911 asking for help and also verify that the telecommunicator works for a 911 PSAP. These verifications take time as they involve faxing and numerous phone calls.

Ten minutes later I was armed with information about the phone location. However, the accuracy wasn't great because the phone was turned off. It most likely died. The location provided was based on the last tower ping, which was not especially helpful. After relaying this to my commander, he asked me to call a long list of resources, and the manpower was short. Additionally, in thirty minutes the IT team was scheduled to completely take down CAD for a bug fix. Without CAD, we wouldn't be able to track anything using our computer software, meaning we had to go old-school and do it all by hand. My team joined me in attempting to make all the notifications before the CAD would be down.

We dove in. I began with the fire department, as their heat signature devices would come in handy. Next, I called a neighboring agency to determine if their police helicopter was cleared to fly. Despite the cold temperatures and the wind, the bird could be flown. Ask and you shall receive! Done. The third request included activating the rescue patrol. I again called fire and rescue to dispatch the team. The last notification on my commander's laundry list was for the office of emergency management. Their efforts would be necessary if deputies weren't able to locate Dillon. However, this request was tricky due to an out-of-date call schedule and the internet being down. The outage had officially begun. CAD was next. Fighting through the outage and apologizing to some really cranky people who weren't on call, I finished the notification.

By this time two deputies had thoroughly combed the area where the cell phone last pinged. Driving up and down the road slowly and traversing what land they could with their patrol cars, they could not find Dillon. Fire and rescue joined the efforts with the fancy heat signature equipment without success. The equipment required warmer temperatures to properly function.

Dillon, where are you?

At six o'clock in the morning, the dayshift began to filter in. The coffee pot started brewing, and their eager chatter reminded me that I needed my bed. After briefly telling the next crew about the call's status (Dillon hadn't been located but was out there freezing his felon butt off), I breathed a sigh of relief. *Thank God.* The last hour and a half of the shift was hell, and my nerve endings were toast. I always knew I needed to be done when I started getting snippy.

Later that day I checked my email to see if Dillon had been found. I quickly located the special report, anticipating dialogue about locating his body. Much to my surprise, at ten o'clock in the morning deputies had located him alive in a grain silo. Rescue personnel treated him for acute hypothermia and then transported him to the jail on his warrant. The end.

So ends the story about Dillon and the strangest, coldest manhunt ever. Throughout that winter, we talked about Dillon often. His story lived in infamy as we recalled trying to save him without internet and working with pen and paper. Thanks, Dillon!

Emma

The year 2021 was interesting for my husband and me. We went on several trips. My team chastised me for going on multiple "vacations," but the majority of our travel was not for pleasure. The first "vacation" was a road trip across the country to join my family in honoring my mother's passing. We also flew to North Carolina and then drove with family to Dothan, Alabama, to attend the funeral for our grandpa, who died of COVID-19. After all this, I finally enjoyed some relaxing vacation time in Jamaica with friends, in the Colorado mountains for my birthday, and in San Antonio for our tenth anniversary.

Ironically, during these trips I called 911 three times. Although I was desperately trying to get away from work and catch a breather, work was haunting me.

The first time occurred on our trip to the mountains surrounding Gunnison. As a tradition, we make the trek west multiple times a year, always once around my birthday because summertime in the mountains is my happy place. As we were sitting and planning the hours of activities before camping, someone mentioned the rodeo was in town. In the spirit of "going with the flow," we bought tickets and headed to Tough Enough To Wear Pink night at Cattleman's Days.

We splurged to get the grandstand seating to avoid sitting in the sun. The heat can truly be unbearable. After finding our row and grabbing our seats, I surveyed our group and was humbled to be among such amazing humans. Four of us were serving in law enforcement: two police officers, a dispatch supervisor, a corrections officer, and with us were the wife and child of a police officer. Birds of a feather really do flock together. Anyone looking at us would never know our professions; we typically do not like to stand out in crowds.

As the sun started to set and the rodeo began, we stood for the national anthem, which was sung live and broadcast loud enough to hear miles away. About three-quarters of the way through the performance, a huge *slam!*

shook the bleachers a few rows behind us. My husband, who was seated closest to the sound and had the best visual, turned to me and shouted, "Call 911 for a girl having a seizure!" I didn't waste time and switched into dispatch supervisor mode.

"911, what's the address of the emergency?" The words shook me from this side of the phone.

Anticipating the telecommunicator's questions and needs, I started screaming information into the phone, trying to be louder than the performance in the background.

"HI, WE'RE IN THE GRANDSTANDS OF THE RODEO. A GIRL IS SEIZING! I DON'T KNOW HER. SHE LOOKS TO BE A TEENAGER," I shouted as loud as I could.

I knew the dispatcher's voice. She was one of my ride-or-dies when I worked for emergency services in the Gunnison area. Afterward, we would share a laugh and apologize for screaming at one another, but this was not the time.

As I was having a screaming match over the national anthem (what is it with me and the national anthem?), my husband was instructing family members while our group ran to find emergency personnel at the rodeo. They quickly located on-duty police officers and an EMS crew and brought them straight to the incident.

Help had arrived, and the patient was further treated in a medical tent. After all was said and done, our group went back to sitting in the bleachers, watching the rodeo. We removed our on-duty hats as quickly as we had put them on. Seemingly we had attracted some attention; a group of middle-aged ladies came up to us and commented on our swift action and bravery. They thanked us and discussed how smart and incredibly impressed they were. Truth be told, that was the first sincere, in-person "thank you" I have ever received for being in emergency services.

A couple of weeks later a quick getaway with my husband for our tenth anniversary, I called 911 again. We had wanted to go somewhere we hadn't been before, but we also didn't want to break the bank, so we traveled to San Antonio to visit the acclaimed Riverwalk and the Alamo, which appeased the history nerd I married.

The day we left, I couldn't miss a scheduled training, so I had booked a later flight to avoid taking any more time off than needed. And the day was stacked. My itinerary would have easily been ruined if one thing went wrong; everything was planned to the minute.

1. Leave at 3:00 p.m.

2. Drive to the airport, missing rush hour.

3. Arrive at the airport one and a half to two hours before our flight, leaving a little room for checking bags and going through security.

4. Board the plane at 6:00 p.m.

5. Check into the hotel.

6. Relax and enjoy a late dinner.

Can you tell I'm an over planner? *Remember I am blue!* I thrive in the details but experience significant anxiety when things don't go as planned.

The day arrived, and steps one through three were perfectly completed. We got to the airport, checked in for our flight, then headed toward security—always the wild card. As we wound through the maze at Denver International Airport, we were making good time. As we approached the final U-turn in the queue, out of the corner of my eye I saw a girl right behind me pass out. *Boom!* She hit the deck hard. My husband, again quick to action, knelt to help her, while a bystander barked, "Call 911!"

I made eye contact with her with my phone already in hand. "I got it!" I answered. *Here we go again.*

My call was answered by a recording. "Hi, you have reached Denver 911. Do not hang up. All call takers are currently busy."

What is this? At our center, we strive to answer every 911 call in under ten seconds, an accomplishment we take pride in. For all high-priority (threat to life) calls, we have a standard of dispatched officers arriving on scene in less than five minutes. A 911 call answered by a recording illustrates the staffing crisis that plagues most PSAPs.

Annoyed and rolling my eyes, I committed the cardinal sin of a 911 caller: I hung up the phone. NEVER HANG UP. Logically I reasoned that I never spoke to an actual person, so how could they call me back? And maybe I could find help on-scene faster, as we did at the rodeo. Nonetheless, the robot called me back and reminded me that I shouldn't have hung up.

Tethered to this process, I put the phone on speaker, knowing it would take a while. In the meantime, my husband rolled the patient over, got her legs crossed, and sat her up in the recovery position. I helped him in his triage by getting on the ground and asking her name and some other questions from the EMD protocol I had committed to memory.

"Hi, what's your name?" I started simply.

"Chloe," she offered.

"Hi, Chloe. I'm Emma. We're getting you help. Just take some deep breaths for me—in through your nose and out through your mouth. Do that five times, OK?" She complied with my instructions.

"Did you hit your head?" I continued. Uncertain and clearly in shock, she didn't answer. We focused again on breathing.

In the meantime, the TSA agents used their radios to request medical assistance. Medics quickly arrived, and I provided them an assessment of the situation. As I resumed moving up in the security queue, my phone played hold music on speaker. Finally, I got a call-taker. I explained that I had called for medical attention in security, but help was on scene. She thanked me for my patience and allowed me to hang up.

A couple of weeks after our trip to San Antonio, we went to Alabama for our grandfather's funeral. The logistics of organizing everyone who wanted to go and how to get everyone together were challenging. In the end, my husband, his brother (also an officer), and I all flew to North Carolina. There we picked up my mother-in-law and drove for eight more hours to Dothan, Alabama, while other family members caravanned behind us the entire time—six people in two cars. Our car was a riot. When my brother-in-law and I get together, we bicker like actual siblings (in good fun, of course). Thirty minutes together is enough time to suffice for a long while. Naturally, three days of traveling together was chaos.

The first half of the trip went as well as it could. Lots of driving, very little sleep, emotions all over the place. After the funeral, we decided to leave immediately and drive back to North Carolina. Alabama was in the hot zone for COVID-19 at the time, so we did not want to spend any more time there than necessary.

We started our drive around one in the afternoon. After a few hours of driving, I told my brother-in-law that I needed to use the bathroom. In the middle of nowhere, we had a hard time finding a gas station. My husband was sleeping, and my mother-in-law was in the front seat. He and I argued about where to pull over, and I looked on my phone and found a couple of options a few miles up the road. After confirming with the caravan car behind us, we all agreed to stop.

My very protective, paranoid, safety-oriented, always-on-the-lookout, strait-laced law enforcement brother-in-law pulled over to the shadiest-looking gas station I have ever seen. Meanwhile, there was a normal gas station ACROSS THE STREET. *Whatever.* I rolled my eyes. When a girl's gotta go, a girl's gotta go. As I ran inside to use the bathroom, I heard a distinct crash. But too focused on my own mission to relieve myself, I trudged on. Touching as little as possible, I made it through the experience.

When I walked back to the car, I noticed a lot of commotion. All the passengers stood with angry expressions outside their vehicles, and a crowd gathered to lobby in the who-hit-whom game. In the middle of all of the commotion was our second caravan car with noticeable damage to their front bumper. Knowing my family was not familiar with these types of situations, I stepped up and encouraged my sister-in-law to call 911 while her brothers monitored the motor vehicle accident situation. I helped her out, coaching her to give the dispatcher the following information:

1. The name of the gas station,

2. Her contact information, especially her call-back number,

3. A short description of what occurred,

4. Good details, including the license plate of the other vehicle involved. The driver had initially tried to leave the scene, so I knew something was fishy, and the plate might come in handy.

My sister-in-law was able to answer the rest of the telecommunicator's questions on her own, and in a few short minutes, an officer was on scene. In the end, the subject who hit our family's car ended up going to jail for an outstanding arrest warrant.

These three instances gave me a very real glimpse into what it is like on the other side of the phone. I realized that there is terror and fear, even for a trained professional in emergency services! I was happy to know that in each of these circumstances, I was able to affect real change and use my powers for good. Right place, right time.

Lea

Ihad worked on the job for just shy of eight years before I had my first homicide call. Many of my coworkers handled several during their careers, including a call from a man who described how he had just stabbed his roommate to death, and another who had suffocated his brother after a family fight. Both cool as cucumbers, calling on emergency lines and detailing their murderous actions. Before one April night, I had never had a call where someone else killed another person.

"911, where is your emergency?"

"I was stabbed in the head. . .oh my god!" a male screamed, huffing and puffing.

Another telecommunicator interjected. "This is Denver with a transfer, I am getting a strong cell phone location in your town. He is talking about a male possible assault with a weapon," she said, announcing a transfer and giving me a little more detail than the caller had originally provided.

"OK, did you get an address?" I asked, speaking to the telecommunicator.

"I did not. Wanted to bring you on as quickly as possible and let you figure it out," she said. I was initially very frustrated with this laziness. Phone locations can often be very misleading, and I never transferred a call until I had confirmed a location. Clearly, I was going to do the heavy lifting yet again.

"Thank you. OK, caller?" I was done with her ineptitude. "Sir, what address are you at?" I asked. He panted and breathed heavily on the phone. I deduced the caller had been running.

"Sir, hello?" I offered again. More heavy breathing, and his phone shifted loudly in my ear. "Hello, are you there?"

"Yeah, I am here!" he yelled. "He had a gun, and he stabbed me in the head." I took a second to process and take a deep breath, then I started typing.

"Somebody stabbed you?" I repeated for his clarification while simultaneously alerting my shift mates to perk up and get ready to work.

"Robbed the house. Everything." He breathed heavily between each word. "I said goodbye to him. . ." His errant thought trailed off. Perhaps the head wound was talking?

"I need to know the address, please. Do you know where you are?" I pleaded.

There was no answer. The Denver telecommunicator was still on the line, surprisingly, and offered an address per her phone history. I also pulled up phone history and used RapidSOS to see if I could ascertain a location. The location indicated by his phone ping and the address associated with his phone were blocks apart and both in my police jurisdiction. With this narrowed down, I dismissed the Denver telecommunicator, picked an address, and dropped in a call for dispatch. Scant notes included "unknown exact address of occurrence; caller saying he was stabbed; unknown assailants had a gun; male, probable head wound."

I realized this wasn't a ton of information, but the call needed to be dispatched. As I dropped the call for service in the queue, Amber, operating Channel One, started a quick and direct dispatch. Using the address my CAD associated with the phone number, I checked the premise history. Several calls appeared, many of which involved domestic violence disputes and drugs. According to the information I collected, the subject's name should be Brayden. Armed with a little more information, I called him back. The phone rang twice and then picked up. Silence.

"Hello?" I started. "Brayden, are you there?" This gained his immediate attention. Calling someone by their name tends to do that.

"Yes." He was still huffing and puffing.

"This is 911 calling you back. Are you at Harvard or Roslyn?" I said bluntly. His phone was pinging on Harvard, but the historical data for his phone number indicated his address should be on Roslyn. I continued to battle the inaccurate cell phone location. I needed clarification on the address before I did anything else.

"I'm on Roslyn," he choked.

"OK, Brayden, are you outside? Or are you inside your apartment at number 1805?" I'm sure my knowing so much seemed creepy, but he didn't appear to mind.

"I'm inside at 1805," he stated. Perfect. I knew exactly where he was, so I changed the address to reflect it.

"Very good. I have help on the way to you! They are coming as fast as they can," I said reassuringly.

"He came with a gun, and she stabbed me in the head," he volunteered. Two assailants. Call history indicated some beef with an ex-girlfriend.

"Who is this? A girlfriend?" I shifted my questioning in that direction.

"Huh?" He sounded surprised. "Yes, my ex."

"She stabbed you in the head. Are you bleeding?" I continued the questions.

"Yes," he stated.

I could hear Amber phoning rescue to update them about the call. I didn't transfer the call to them because I needed call control to continue gathering information about suspects. I saw my other partner adding information to the narrative about the ex-girlfriend with her name and DOB. This was teamwork at its best.

"Where is she right now?" I clarified, knowing this would change a few things about the responding unit's plan of attack.

"He had a gun. I had to get away from them." He was having a hard time focusing, and I was having a hard time hearing him.

"Did these people leave, Brayden?" I tried to refocus him on the present.

No answer. Just a lot of heavy breathing.

"Brayden, I have help coming to you as quickly as possible. Is that female still there or did she leave?" Full court press here.

"You got someone coming? OK." He sounded relieved. I think the blood loss and shock were working against any progress I hoped to make on this call.

"I've got help coming. I just need to know where she is." Fourth time is a charm, maybe?

"I'm at my house. . ." then he started to rattle off the address again. I was stuck in a loop with a very terrified man.

"No, no, no," I interrupted, "where is SHE?" I was hoping vocal emphasis would help.

"I'm at home. . ." *Oh jeez, Louise! Brayden!*

"Where are THEY?" I asked about the assailants again.

"I'm not sure. Not sure if they were leaving or what they were doing," he advised. OK, this gave me something.

"You are at your house safe, though?" I tried a different angle.

"I am," he stated with as much confidence a man can muster after being brutally attacked in his own home.

"Anyone drinking?" I started with a standard line of questions we ask on all calls.

"I had a few beers earlier today," he stated.

"Anyone using any drugs?"

"No, no drugs," he offered.

Before I could ask my next question, a large dog started barking in the background.

"Come on in, y'all," he screamed, intuition telling him they were the good guys. Help had arrived.

"Brayden, that is my deputy. I am going to let you go," I stated.

"Dasha, come here, girl! Come here!" He attempted to wrangle his dog. I disconnected.

Blue in the face from asking where his assailants were so many times, I hung up knowing help had arrived in good time. Soon my deputies advised that rescue was clear for entry and the scene was safe. Brayden had a serious head laceration and a very swollen eye that needed attention. He was transported to a nearby hospital for further care. A deputy followed the ambulance to the hospital so he could continue questioning Brayden. This deputy soon relayed the exact names and ages of the suspects and where they should be located. They were arrested and charged with attempted homicide over the next two days.

Unfortunately, this story is not an uncommon one. Brayden lived with his on-again, off-again girlfriend of three years, Kay, at the Roslyn address. Earlier that day, while Brayden was working, Kay relaxed at their apartment with her "male friend," Kyle. She was having a hard time and had asked Kyle to come over. He brought the popular pick-me-up, fentanyl. The pair enjoyed their high but craved a change of scenery. So, they went to Kyle's place. Brayden arrived at the apartment after working and noticed that Kay wasn't home. After talking to Kay on the phone, he was worried, so he walked to Kyle's for more information and to bring Kay home. Brayden knocked on the door and was greeted with a Glock in his face. A struggle ensued. Brayden ended up pistol whipped but was able to pin Kyle to the couch, so Kay stabbed Brayden in the head with a kitchen knife.

Amidst the commotion, Brayden wrestled the gun from Kyle, which he threw into the parking lot as he ran back to his house and called 911. Our K9 unit never located the gun. I am convinced there is more to the story because a lot of the details didn't add up. In my professional opinion, this story reeks of a drug deal gone bad. Either way, Brayden got the crappy end of the deal with a bad head laceration and one less girlfriend, but at least he had his life.

vvv

The same week as the attempted homicide, I began my final Saturday night shift during the tail end of a murder-suicide that occurred in a sleepy townhome community in our jurisdiction. I don't know what Kool-Aid everyone was drinking that week, but it was homicide-inducing. Folks in the business call it "murder weather." When it gets crazy hot and the blood boils, people snap.

The temperatures that week busted records. By Saturday's grisly discovery, everyone was ready for a do-over. This call started the previous Saturday when the dayshift received a call to check welfare at the address in question. The caller was the brother of the home occupant. He informed us that he had just gotten off the phone with his brother, and things seemed amiss. His ex-military intuition was highly bothered by his brother's strange statements. He would have checked on him himself but was out of state, so he requested units check in with his brother. Deputies responded and processed a standard check of the home. Blinds were drawn. Nothing seemed out of place or disturbed. A walk around the property yielded no signs of forced entry. There was no answer at the door. The call was cleared out without a report.

Life resumed.

On the following Tuesday, a concerned coworker phoned in and advised that her work friend hadn't attended any of their scheduled virtual meetings.

Granted, things had changed during the pandemic, and a lot of people were working remotely, but she equated this behavior to not even showing up for work. There had been a big meeting and presentation they were supposed to do together on Monday, and her coworker didn't show. She called, emailed, and texted. Nothing. According to their manager, the female hadn't logged any work activity for two days, which was very odd behavior for this high achiever. History at the address revealed it was the same house that deputies had checked on Saturday. Insert eyebrow raise here. Deputies went out again to the townhome on Tuesday, making sure to walk around the residence and knock on the door. No answer, no movement, nothing. Aside from one package at the front door, there was still nothing unusual. Another call for service cleared out with a "no report."

On Saturday night I walked into work at eight thirty and noted unusual activity. Saturday afternoons were typically tame; normally the world didn't blow up until the graveyard shift walked in to deal with the destructive drunks. I glanced at the CAD screen and saw a lot of cars on duty. Many more than usual. Additionally, they all looked like they were attached to one call, which spelled trouble.

As I walked back to my office, one of my coworkers informed me they had a murder-suicide in sleepy Precinct 3. My face contorted with consternation, and she laughed, confirming the news. First of all, murder-suicides were rare. Also, Precinct 3? No. Precinct 3 is for mail theft, traffic complaints, and neighbor disagreements. *What the heck?*

I signed in and started helping immediately. Reading through the call to familiarize myself, I could see that it originated as a message. The ex-military brother had called in that morning advising he had spoken to a neighbor (Man! He was doing his homework! Not your average citizen. I'm picturing Liam Neeson in *Taken*). The neighbor had heard a loud bang a couple of days ago, and the brother asked if this new information garnered reasonable cause to go inside the house and check. A deputy called him and added notes stating

RP is out of state. Getting very worried. His brother lives here with 10-96 issues. Mail is piling up. Two loud bangs were heard nearby, and RP hasn't been in contact with brother or his wife since a week ago, Saturday. RP is military and fearing for the worst—murder-suicide. Requesting we make more attempts to check welfare on subjects.

After those notes were entered, another caller phoned in, advising she was the boss of the female resident who hadn't shown up to work all week. The boss was at the residence checking her employee's welfare and wanted police assistance because a dog was barking incessantly inside, and no one was answering the door. These two successive calls elevated the call type from a message to a welfare check. Deputies arrived on scene at five o'clock. A short fifty minutes later, a case number was requested, along with investigation supervisors and a victim advocate.

In the fifty minutes that deputies were on scene with the work supervisor, they again checked around the residence and knocked on the door. No one answered. They tried to contact the landlord for the property without an answer. Then a rather ingenious deputy noticed a large AC unit on the back side of the townhome. He stood on the unit and stretched his arm with his phone to a skylight window and took a picture. When he looked at his phone, the picture revealed a ghastly sight in the living room. Two deceased people lay on the couch, one far more decomposed than the other.

This confirmation started a chain reaction within the department to get a warrant to enter the property. Because the occupants were deceased, deputies couldn't just bust down the door. There was no threat to life or property since the subjects were already dead. After a rush warrant was issued to enter the property, the work began on the crime scene.

My deputy friend later told us about the incident. He said it smelled just like you think it would. Nasty. The dog was fine, thank God. The female's death was caused by a single shot from a shotgun. She was probably watching TV on the couch when he came to the loft balcony and shot her. It was evident the female had been killed well before the male due to her level of decompensation. Investigators presume he shot her Saturday or Sunday, then hung out, watched TV, and went about his life, probably contemplating what he was going to do. Investigators found receipts in the kitchen indicating he got an oil change on the car Monday, so he likely he killed himself Monday night or Tuesday by rigging the same shotgun to shoot himself right next to his partner's decomposing body.

From the call history and the brother's insight, we learned that the male struggled with many mental health issues. *Clearly.* I don't know any sane person who kills someone and then hangs out for a few days living in the same space as a decomposing body.

I asked the deputy to show me the pictures of the crime scene. (Telecommunicators are kind of sick in that way.) Years later, I can still remember that picture perfectly. Two bodies lying on a green couch at opposite angles. The female's face was dark and ashen from the blood pooling due to gravity. Her mouth was open with a scream-like face. The male was similarly posed, his mouth also agape. On the other couch sat a small white dog, who probably best understood the exact events that transpired, a silent witness.

At the end of the day, people lost those they love, and that is the saddest thing of all. If you or someone you know is struggling with mental health issues, please do not suffer in silence or let your loved ones suffer. Get help. Below is one of the many resources available for those who are suffering themselves or for loved ones who need support.

SAMHSA's National Helpline,
1-800-662-HELP (4357)

This is a confidential, free, information service for individuals or family members facing mental and/or substance use disorders, available twenty-four hours a day, 365 days a year. They provide referrals to local facilities, support groups, and community-based organizations.

Lea

The telecommunicator's duties continuously evolve; conversely telecommunicators largely detest change. New technology presents the highest hurdles in a PSAP, bringing large learning curves and frustration. Just when the job seems impossible, an unceasing revolving door of technology is the cherry on top of a poop sundae.

During my career, the pervasive nature of social media dramatically accelerated. I started my service when Facebook was booming, then came Instagram, Snapchat, TikTok, and a plethora of other platforms that connected people from across the globe. Great in theory, but it could get very tricky within emergency services. For example, one night in the middle of a frenzy of high-priority calls, a Text-to-911 rang in. I clicked on the incoming messages to find a novel detailing how the texter followed a girl on TikTok, and this subject had just posted a "goodbye" message. After her post, she deleted all her other posts. The texter was very concerned. In messaging with her and asking the standard questions, I needed to enter a wellness check call for service, but she provided me nothing. NOT A THING. Social media has advanced our society in many ways, but in this instance, it was a major setback.

I paused for a minute. I needed to let this call marinate; I had never dealt with this kind of "where in the world" before. Normally I would have a name or a phone number to start digging with, but I was armed with exactly nothing in this instance. If I don't have an address, I would normally get a name and date of birth and do a "Query Driver Alpha" in the state system to see if the person we needed to check had been issued a driver's license. That driver's license could give me an address and a place to start. But on this night, I had no name and no DOB. Sometimes I could get a phone number and use that to cross-reference and find a name or address associated. No phone number. All she had was a TikTok username. Without any of this information, I turned my attention to a few other priority items while this cooked on the back burner of my mind.

After I completed my other tasks, I checked to see if TikTok had an emergency service customer service person I could contact. Fortuitously, they did. It was an email. This wasn't my favorite way to communicate, especially at four in the morning; however, I knew this was my only option. I gave it a shot. I quickly typed an introduction and summarized the situation and what information I was seeking. I got an email back ten minutes later.

Thank you for contacting us. We received your request. This email is for sworn law enforcement agency use only. Any emails submitted from non-sworn law enforcement agencies will not be responded to.

And that was it—a canned response when someone's life was at stake. At this point, twenty minutes into the texting conversation, my RP was getting antsy. She called 911. I answered her call, luckily, and spared her the task of repeating the details. I reassured her I was working on the issue. I disclosed that I had to go through TikTok for information and was waiting on them. Unfortunately, I didn't have an update and couldn't provide a time frame for a welfare check. She was discouraged. The process took so long. Too long. Long enough to make a hasty yet permanent decision. Despite this, she thanked me and hung up the phone.

Five minutes later, a TikTok representative called. I relayed all the details I knew about the situation and the information my RP had provided.

"For the information you need, ma'am, a sworn member of your agency will have to put in a request via a form I will email to you. I cannot process this request because you are just a dispatcher," she replied, effectively slapping me across the face.

The tangible lack of respect toward a first responder working hand-in-hand with other first responders in emergency services was offensive. On top of that, the TikTok process requiring a sworn member of the agency was completely counterintuitive. At this point in the call for service, who knew more details about this incident, me or a deputy? Without a breath to argue, I told her to email me the form, and I called the first available deputy I found. I didn't have to plead for help after reviewing the situation over the phone. My deputy advised she would fill out the form and get the information needed right away.

I left work thirty minutes later for a week on vacation. After returning, I asked my deputy what happened with this incident. She informed me that after emailing the form, she received a generic response from TikTok, advising the threat had already been reported, and the appropriate law enforcement agency had been notified. The end.

I struggled with the lack of closure. *Who was this girl? Where was she? Did she get help? Did she need help? Was this a prank?* Questions flooded my brain. This call represents thousands of other calls during my career that I took without knowing the ending. I am not alone in this feeling of emptiness. I know Emma and a host of other telecommunicators battle with this daily. Technology has only increased the phenomenon of ambiguity that deeply affects not only those in the telecommunicator chair. This call involved my deputy, my RP, myself, and my teammates—all of us sharing this experience without knowing the outcome. And the ripples expand from there.

Lea

Eight years into my dispatching career I distinctly felt the thrill wearing off. The armor I wore to work every day was rusted. The proverbial hat I donned for every shift was old and tattered. It became too easy to forget details, names, and the horrors I listened to each day. All the calls ran together, and I felt my heart harden and my soul becoming jaded. When I started, I thought I would never get to that point. But somehow with a lifetime of horrible experiences consolidated into eight short years, it happened. I finally reached the breaking point.

When I sat down to work that night, I was already ready to go home. I had adjusted my hours for Thursday's graveyard shift for an earlier start in a vain attempt to get more sleep before my vacation the following day. I was severely vacation starved—in six months I had only taken two days. I was getting antsy to be free of the center and off my graveyard schedule. The universe had different plans, and at four o'clock as I was about to bid adieu to this seemingly uneventful day, several 911s suddenly rang in. *Noooooooooooooooo*. I couldn't abandon my team and leave them high and dry. Not my style. I begrudgingly tore my eyes away from the clock, deserting the idea of packing up, and clicked into the first 911 call.

"911, where is your emergency?" I asked, annoyance peppering my voice.

"Um, 97009 East Gage Avenue," she stumbled. After hearing her fourteen-year-old voice, I knew I would have to put my irritated tone to rest so I could be the first responder she needed. I also knew I wasn't leaving anytime soon.

"97009 East Gage Avenue at the Redfern Inn?" I interjected.

"Yes, ma'am," she said meekly.

"What is going on there?" I asked.

"My stepdad came in while I was checking my mom's laundry and locked me out of my room. Now he is sitting in there yelling and threatening her. I am scared for her!" she sobbed. I pinpointed the room number with her.

"Yes," she affirmed, "and he has a gun with him," she volunteered. My attention was fully present, and I zoned in with laser focus.

"What is his name? And what is your mom's name?" I continued, trying to get as much information as possible.

She answered both through tears. I attempted to counsel her a little, advising her I had help started and needed her to take a deep breath.

"What are they arguing about?" I asked.

"My stepdad is accusing her of cheating," she replied.

I got her name and confirmed her phone number appearing on my screen. Other lines kept ringing in—the center was very busy. I had to put her on hold several times to answer incoming lines.

"I have a deputy on the way. Has anyone been drinking today?" I circled back to her after putting a line on hold.

"I don't know for sure. My mom definitely hasn't. She is pregnant." I heard this and was reminded of a shocking statistic: pregnant women are the most at-risk population in the country for violence.

"Any drugs at all?" I continued my questions.

"I don't know. May have been cocaine use?" she stammered.

"Does he normally use cocaine?" I inquired.

"Sometimes, yeah. Off and on," she added with shame.

"Is he associated with a car?" My mind was checking off a mental list of questions needed for gathering good information. I am a beast at getting the details. She gave me the necessary facts, apologizing for not knowing the license plate. Despite being fourteen and terrified, she was a great RP.

"Do they fight often?" I continued.

"Yeah, but I think he is just high, and he is scaring me because he has a gun. He pointed it at her." *Lovely*, I thought. If that is true, there would be solid charges for felony menacing.

"He pointed it at her?" I reiterated.

"Yes," she said with certainty. We fleshed out more details about the fight.

"We have help on the way. Take a deep breath and know they are coming. You did the right thing by calling." My voice was softer delivering these instructions. I had fully accepted that I was not leaving on time as I had hoped. I was right where I was meant to be.

Just then another of my coworkers got a call from a guest on the second floor of the same hotel. This RP reported hearing loud arguing and a gunshot. Seeing this new narrative populate my call queue, I redirected my line of questioning.

"Are you in a safe place?" I asked.

"I am in the front lobby. I am OK." Her sobs ended, and she stood resolute, playing her part in a heinous situation. We discussed descriptions of her parents, and I continued to reassure her. My deputies arrived shortly after we fleshed out that information. She thanked me for my help, and I felt a twinge of guilt for my gruff demeanor earlier in the call.

It was not long before Channel One initiated emergency traffic for all the deputies associated with this call. As they approached the room, the smell of gunpowder and the sight of shell casings on the ground told a story that required extra units and complete focus. Quickly, deputies deduced the room was quiet. Despite this, evacuations were needed for safety. The entire hotel was woken up before daybreak to vacate the premises.

As the evacuations were underway, other deputies reviewed camera footage with the hotel staff. They came to realize that the people matching the description had left using the back stairs just as deputies arrived. The interaction and body language between the two looked forced and violent. The female fashioned a bleeding head wound. Armed with this information, deputies forced entry into the hotel room. Empty. With this discovery, deputies on scene requested telecommunicators to start calling local hospitals and inquire about a female with a head laceration, possibly due to a gunshot wound. Nothing turned up, but all the nurses took our information. Additionally, the on-scene sergeant requested a phone ping. Also, we needed to enter the vehicle into the state system and issue a BOLO for other local agencies. These activities within the center required a lot of time and attention, and each telecommunicator performed a task while simultaneously fielding incoming calls. I even had a telecommunicator working during her break to assist the team.

For two hours we worked on this call. Worked the crap out of it. I was impressed with my team's rigor, attention to detail, and synergy.

Everything calmed down for a moment, and my acting supervisor turned her chair to look at me. "Go! You may not get another chance," she said sympathetically, citing my twelve-hour shift. With this blessing, I bolted.

When I checked in with my team the next day, I was happy to hear that they had not been busy after I left and that the injured mom walked into the hotel ten minutes after I ran out the door. The male and the car were nowhere to be found. She refused to cooperate with the police and insisted she didn't want to press charges. She only wanted to speak with her daughter, but she did acquiesce to a paramedic tending to her intense head wound without law enforcement present. Despite the mom's lack of cooperation, good charges were established for the male suspect, and a BOLO was issued for his car. A couple of days later, a neighboring agency found the vehicle and our suspect. He was arrested. Hopefully, this allowed mom and daughter some peace away from a violent predator.

While this knowledge of a job well done confirmed my purpose and gave me a boost of career confidence, thoughts of doubt simmered beneath the surface because of the emotional burnout I felt. While I lackadaisically dipped my foot in a kiddie pool and sipped on a beer while relaxing with family, my restless mind wandered, contemplating my future as a telecommunicator. Little did I know in three months' time I would be writing my letter of resignation and hanging up my headset forever.

Lea

There is a phenomenon called "dispatch priming." Telecommunicators can inadvertently adjust a response to a call for service based on the content of their questioning and radio communication. With the information relayed, they can negatively "prime" a situation before an officer gets on scene. For example, a telecommunicator could air an alarm at a residence and include historical information, such as domestic violence incidents with weapons involved. An officer responding would now know that it could be more than a routine residential alarm, thus coaching them to make judgment calls beyond what is necessary.

Just like a journalist trying to report on an issue while excluding their voice or opinions, a telecommunicator must try to remain objective. However, we are not objective. We are humans! We have experiences that pepper our decision-making and help guide us. Our training teaches us to filter our bias and obtain the facts. Gather information and report the caller's experience through good and consistent questioning, utilizing our instincts and critical thinking skills to light the path. Easy, right? Not every call hits the mark. I have one call that still haunts me and is a good example of dispatch priming based on my personal knowledge and experiences.

I am a huge *Dateline* fan, and one stunning episode explored the Kalamazoo, Michigan, rideshare killing spree. In February 2016, an average Joe spent a normal day taxiing multiple passengers for a popular rideshare program. Sporadically throughout his ten hours in the car, he shot his passengers. Between these moments of psychosis, he would pick up and safely deliver other patrons. By the end of the day, he had randomly selected and shot eight people, killing five of them. This story opened my eyes to the dangers of ridesharing. The internet tells thousands of stories about passengers being raped, killed, kidnapped, battered, sexually harassed, and injured by their rideshare drivers. With that knowledge in the back of my brain during the summer of 2021, I took a 911 call.

"911, what is the address of your emergency?" I said as enthusiastically as I could muster at one in the morning and running on four hours of sleep.

"Yeah, I am actually riding with a Lyft driver, and I am asking him to pull over, and he won't. He is not listening to me. He is ignoring me. What can I do about that?" a seemingly sober male asked without panic.

"Where are you?" I deadpanned.

"We are on what looks like Havana Street. Big Creek, maybe?" he replied. I cross-checked the map to validate his assumptions. I still needed more.

"Um, passing a Shell station?" he offered. Bingo. Knowing the exact location, I dropped in the call after fifteen seconds of initial triage. Kidnapping, which is a Priority One call for service. It blinked red in the queue. Mallory dispatched with alert tones, starting the priming process. Our deputies began to respond with lights and sirens. Everyone fed off a collective adrenaline rush.

"We are getting out right here at the red light," he told me.

I can faintly hear a female voice in the background, pleading to be let out.

"Let us out, we want to go," my RP echoed.

"What is your name?" I asked to keep him engaged.

"Jason. He is letting us out right now," he said with a sigh.

"The driver let you out?" I confirmed.

"Yes, we did get out," Jason offered. I updated the call but still heard sirens blowing past them. I knew units were close.

The female in the background offered the vehicle plate and description. After running the license plate, I discovered it matched the description of the vehicle. I added this information to my call for service. My RP continued to talk about how the driver completely ignored them. I let him ramble while I entered information. I heard Mallory put the main channel on emergency as deputies initiated a traffic stop with the suspect vehicle.

"What did the driver look like?" I asked, continuing to gather information for my deputies.

"Cuban. Light skinned, short curly hair," Jason offered.

"Which direction did he go?" This question found Jason and me fuddling through an amateur tango, leading me to believe he was less sober than I originally thought. More sirens blared through the phone. Finally, a responding deputy arrived at Jason's location, relieving me from duty. I hung up the phone and focused on the radio traffic. I overheard units communicating about pulling over the driver for a traffic stop. The driver was taken out of the vehicle at gunpoint. Tension was thick in the room as we waited with bated breath. Moments later a C4 status allowed us to breathe deeply. Emergency traffic on Channel One was lifted, and I immediately texted my friend on the road and asked him to call in. I needed to hear the story!

He made me wait. An hour later he called with a twist I didn't see coming. As it turned out, the driver was deaf. A sign posted in his car, albeit hard to see, explained this and instructed passengers on how to communicate with him. The not-so-sober passengers missed the detail, hence the 911 kidnapping call. *Yikes.* That was a gut punch. Thankfully the driver was not too upset. As deputies scribbled notes back and forth with him, he was very understanding about the situation.

That didn't stop my team from harassing me all night about this call. All night. ALL NIGHT! They joked with me about all the call types I could have chosen that would have been more appropriate. Suspicious circumstances. Welfare check.

"Heck, even a follow-up would have been better!" Mallory ribbed me amid my tears of laughter. Reflecting, I see how my knowledge of rideshare horrors skewed my interpretation of this call.

However, I still stand by my decision to put the call in as a kidnapping. In dispatch there is a saying, *you are only as good as your RP.* Telecommunicators act solely based on the information presented to them. In this circumstance, two not-entirely-sober people told me they were being kidnapped in a vehicle. I don't believe in coincidence or chance. I was the one who was meant to pick up that call. The situation was supposed to happen the way it did. If anything, it taught me that I may need to get out of the game, sooner than later. Perhaps my spidey senses weren't what they used to be, or maybe the fact that I hadn't slept in over two years was starting to catch up to me. Either way, while my team and I laughed it off that night, I knew deep inside that a major change was on the horizon.

Lea

"**A** red sun rises. Blood has been spilled this night," Legolas utters under his breath, staring at the eastern sky in a classic *Lord of the Rings* scene.[13] These words rang in my ears as I silently drove due east into a rising sun after an officer-involved shooting. The bright red color burned into my mind as I recalled what had happened just six hours prior. A man had been shot and killed by my officers after a standoff. It was one of the worst nights in my career—and one that officially cemented the calling I had been feeling in my heart during the last few months.

It had already been a long week. Nothing crazy or significant, just severely short-staffed. I had three employees out for vacation, funeral leave, and maternity leave. None of the overtime had been picked up, so the day shift was staying late, and graveyards were coming in early to meet minimum staffing. We all took turns working twelve-hour shifts. Additionally, I was in the middle of the two busiest weeks leading our PSAP public education team. When I was promoted to supervisor, I took over the position of public education coordinator and had the pleasure and pain of coordinating a year's worth of events. I loved it, but the summer was stacked with neighborhood movie nights, block parties, and community gatherings that left me and my team stretched thin. That day I left home early to gather supplies from another local PSAP for a weekend of events. On top of that, I had been planning and hosting my daughter's second birthday. I think I may have slept eight hours in three days. Soldiering on through party planning, overtime, and no sleep, we finally made it to Saturday! Our team breathed a collective sigh of relief knowing this was the last shift of the week for our side of the house.

I walked into work, immediately irritated because I saw that none of my swing shifters had taken a break despite ample staffing. *Lovely.* This rendered me with no time to prepare public education swag for the upcoming events because I needed to cover the floor so folks could take their breaks. I sat down to relieve the data channel operator, who kindly left me two emergency warrants to enter. *Extra lovely.*

"They just came in," she said with a shrug.

"Yay." I rolled my eyes. *Whew!* I needed an attitude adjustment, and I knew it! I stretched my fingers and pounded out the warrants. After everyone took their breaks, I squeezed in thirty minutes of office time, which I spent jogging between my office and the workroom. I built up a sweat hustling to open boxes, organize equipment, take inventory, and plan supplies for six events. Happy with my workout, I collected all the items, wheeled them up to the floor, and begrudgingly advised my team I would need some help filling swag bags.

"That is OK! We don't mind helping," Maggie assured me with a smile.

"Really, Lea?" Mallory looked at me with her eyebrow raised, sarcasm drenching her response.

"You know what, Mallory, I don't have time for your sass tonight. You are gonna help and like it!" I replied jokingly. We started the give-each-other-smack dance earlier than usual.

As I sat down at my computer and took a deep breath before starting the next task, I could hear the main radio airing a physical disturbance. Deputies responded with lights and sirens. My spidey senses tingled. I sent the last staff member on her break and settled back to work at the data channel.

"Channel One is on emergency for Frank 61 at 1107," Maggie aired suddenly.

I was now handling radio traffic for the entire county and the requests were immediate. Traffic stop. Clearance on three parties. Contact a keyholder. Community check. Between transmissions I spent time checking all the calls and reading them thoroughly to familiarize myself. I saw nothing pending that was life-threatening and required immediate action, so I began some simple admin tasks. Three minutes into approving overtime hours, I heard an escalated voice on my channel. No words, just a guttural sound. I didn't even hear the request because my brain couldn't process it in a context that made sense. What was familiar was the tone of panic. The next transmission I heard clearly.

"All Precinct 5 cars en route from the sub Code 3," Edward 30 aired over the data channel.

A chasm the length of a football field existed between hearing and comprehending these transmissions. I still had no idea what call this traffic was associated with. I scanned my calls and didn't see an active call for Precinct 5. *Where are they going? Why are they going? What did I miss?*

I took a deep breath, and it hit me. This was not a request for any of my calls. It was for the call on the main radio. My fingers fumbled but finally remembered the correct command to pull up the call. *Boom.* I saw the impetus.

"Shots fired."

My heart sank. At that same moment, the room exploded into activity. The phones rang off the hook because concerned neighbors, hearing the commotion, were incensed. My radio activity increased tenfold with transmissions from cars that were calling en route to the call. They used my radio to share information and to not bog down the main radio with their transmissions. In between their traffic, my watch commander (the highest-ranking deputy in the field) barked requests for mutual aid to be sent to the location. I started an armored vehicle from a sister agency, paged the SWAT team and CIRT, and gathered information about on-call personnel for notifications. Too waterlogged with tasks, I delegated my acting supervisor to help me with the reverse 911 notification necessary to advising residents to stay inside their homes due to police activity.

I paused knowing we needed more help to keep up with the activity. Quickly I hollered at the telecommunicator on break, recalling her to duty. She hastily wrapped up a phone call and then hustled in our direction. Sitting back down at my console, I steadied myself on Channel Two, handling traffic for the entire county. I dispatched calls and processed requests for clearances and entries into the state data system. As phone calls were needed, my teammates anticipated the requests by listening in on my traffic and made the calls for me so I could focus and avoid spreading myself too thin with multitasking. This was teamwork at its best. I paused during a brief lull.

"Great job, guys! Keep it up! Maggie, you are amazing." I encouraged them while checking the narrative for the officer-involved shooting call.

Was anyone hurt? No. I realized then that I knew relatively little about this call. I skimmed it to catch up. Neighborhood block party shenanigans turned sour when several partygoers attempted to stop a very drunk man, wearing a gun on his hip, from getting behind the wheel. A fight broke out. Cops were called, and when they arrived, the male refused to talk and retreated into his garage. He remained uncooperative when deputies attempted to speak to him about what had happened, and he then opened his garage door and started shooting at the deputies. The situation currently remained at a standstill with him in the garage and police outside.

Meanwhile, the requests kept pouring in. The center treaded water, desperately trudging through the heightened volume on radios and phones. Channel Two was insane. Because of my workload, I continued to delegate, which is something I didn't like doing. I preferred maintaining control, and I hesitated to ask my staff for help, knowing they were just as busy. Each time I requested assistance, I quickly navigated through self-judgment and continued through the quicksand of the night.

This incident went on for a long while. Approaching the end of the shift, I asked the swing team to work overtime, and they quickly agreed without hesitation. Their synergy pressed on. I took a break from the action and walked over to my primary radio telecommunicator, the newest person in the room. From everything I overheard, she was calm, controlled, and had the situation well managed. I offered a little more encouragement, and when we finally made eye contact, I could tell she was OK to keep going.

Beep beep beep! An obstinate emergency alarm pierced the eye of the storm. Maggie status-checked the officer through gunfire. C4. *Beep beep beep beep*! Another alarm chimed in. More status checks. C4. *Beep beep beep beep!* C4. More gunfire could be heard. A cat and mouse game continued for about an hour before the SWAT team on scene launched a drone confirming the subject was down. A contact team approached a heap in the garage. He was dead. The standoff was over by two o'clock, and the threat had been eliminated. No officers were injured.

By three o'clock, my adrenaline had worn off, and the rest of the night was pure agony. Amid an eerie quiet, the rest of the call played out. Coroner. CIRT. Many deputies moved to inactive status, pulled from duty because of their part in the shooting. There were no cover cars for any assignments the rest of the shift, so everyone had to lay low. The night came to a screeching halt. I took advantage of the downturn and rallied my team to make public education goodie bags for kids. With eye rolls and groans, my ladies packed crayons, tattoos, and coloring books into bags like champions. We sat around our lazy Susan table making these bags and began to debrief. Slowly and cautiously, we allowed ourselves to process the event. Thankfully a very funny incident with the printer toner cartridge and Mallory's white shirt gave us all a much-needed cathartic laugh. But even this laughter couldn't fix the somber mood.

Logically, the best possible outcome prevailed. The good guys won. The bad guy lost. But what was left? Vivid memories of an automatic weapon discharging in my ear. Panicked voices gearing up for domestic war. An adrenaline plunge so massive that my body felt like it had been hit by a truck. Hard to think. Hard to feel. Hard to do anything. Sinister voices making me doubt my skills, worth, and leadership. I drove home in silence, seeing the red sun rising and feeling agony for the loss of life. I knew one thing for certain: I was leaving emergency services.

Lea

I sat on the phone crying to Emma one day, resolute in my decision to leave the profession I had fallen madly in love with.

"Are you sure you are done with dispatching?" she asked.

"Yes," I answered confidently, tears staining my shirt.

A year of absolute hell predicated this conversation, and my nerves were in crisis mode. In 2020 I was the sibling primarily responsible for taking care of my mom and watching her die slowly in a nursing home. During that year, the community lost trust in the thin blue line with every scandal that arose. It was heartbreaking. The daily challenges of an extremely stressful work environment, compounded with my lack of sleep and the demands of caring for two kids under age three, intensified my struggles with depression and mental health. To top it all off, this excruciating year coincided with a global pandemic!

In early 2021 after the thousandth I-didn't-sleep-and-I-am-just-so-tired argument, my husband came to me and finally said, "I can't do this anymore." I crumbled, knowing he was right. I had this same conversation with myself before this fight exploded. But I had no plan or idea of how to make changes or fix what was so messed up. I felt completely stuck.

I did not immediately think of leaving my career. I knew that four days a week I got inadequate sleep, which made me cranky and irritable and wreaked havoc on my marriage and my life. I first tried to correct this issue with hormone therapy, having heard good things about this treatment, and I thought it might help me with my energy, mood, and sleep cycles. Lab work revealed a nonexistent testosterone level, so my consultant recommended weekly shots. Twelve weeks later, the side effects from the shots were almost as bad as my original symptoms.

This was not the answer. Armed with a hairy lip and a new alto voice, I was approaching the cliff quickly. Sick and tired of being sick and tired. I wanted to thrive! I promised my mom I would thrive. I promised Spencer I would make changes. And I wasn't going to break either of those promises.

Fear consumed me, and after the disastrous hormone therapy, I had no idea how to correct my situation. In that brokenness I did what I knew. I prayed. Much like I had done at the beginning of my career before every shift and especially during the bathroom pep talks following difficult calls, I lifted my soul to Jesus. I prayed every day.

What happened during the next six months was nothing short of a miracle. Lauren Daigle's lyrics from her song "Rescue" masterfully focused my prayers and need for healing:

> *I hear you whisper underneath your breath*
> *I hear your SOS. . .*
> *I will send out an army to find you*
> *In the middle of the darkest night*
>
> *It's true, I will rescue you.*[14]

God rescued me. All these years, I thought I was the one who was saving people. As it turns out, I was the one who needed help. Slowly my heart began to hear a different call. I needed a new job. I needed to chart a new path. I had spent the previous eight years rising through the ranks, kicking ass, and taking names, and now it was time to walk away to make myself whole again.

"Ugh! What a waste!" I exclaimed to Emma through tears.

"It's not a waste. Look at all the people you helped. Look at all the good you did!" my sister rebutted. Her logic usually outweighed her emotion, but at this moment her heart swelled with concern.

"I knew I was done when I took this call a couple of weeks ago," I sobbed, recalling the awful officer-involved shooting. After I told Emma this story, she didn't offer any objections. She saw the telltale signs of compassion fatigue and burnout. She knew this was the right choice, and she was supportive. It meant the world to me to have her blessing to leave a career that we both loved and shared immense passion for. I felt like I was betraying her a little, but she never held me to that guilt.

I made the decision, and I embarked on the craziest thing I have done in my life. I took a path of self-realization and came face-to-face with a decade of wear and tear on my soul. The eternal optimist who began a career as a naive DINK was choosing reinvention for self-preservation. Here I was staring at my future and erasing all the plans I had made. It was terrifying, humbling, and a little bit exhilarating. The thrill seeker in me sensed a tingle of anticipation. Or was that the testosterone talking? Either way, my telecommunicator journey was ending.

I wrote my resignation letter in solitude. After I wrote it, I asked my husband for edits. He sucked out most of the emotion and deemed it ready. I printed it, sealed it in an envelope, and set it on the kitchen counter. I passed by it all weekend. Sometimes it caught my eye and was reassuring. Other times, it took my breath away. I questioned my decision. Sticking to my gut, on Monday morning I texted my communication manager asking to see her the following day. We arranged a morning meeting.

On Tuesday I dropped off my girls for some fun and took the heaviest piece of paper I'd ever held for a drive. I barged into the sheriff's office, passing through the gate with ease. Walking up the steps to the second floor, my hands shook. *What do I say? How do I leave a job I actually like? Why was I doing this again?* My resolution faltered when I placed my key card on the dispatch badge reader and the door clicked open. As I opened the door, familiar faces looked up from consoles and their expressions were left puzzled.

"Hey Lea! What you are doing here?" Penny greeted from the data channel console. Her friendly face reminded me of our many training sessions eight years ago.

"Hey Penny. I'm here for a meeting," I stumbled, nervous about how to explain my presence to trained observers during my coveted day off.

"How's the day?" I managed, shifting focus.

"Easy so far!" she chortled. I returned her smile.

Four steps forward and I peeked into my managers office. She looked up from her desk and motioned for me to come in. I shut the door behind me, and the letter in my hand burned red hot. I sat down and breathed a long sigh, putting the letter on her desk.

"Oh no, I hoped I wasn't right! Gosh darn it, I'm sad to see you go." She gave me a knowing look and met my eyes.

We launched into a brief conversation about priorities and the extreme honor I had serving as a supervisor for the agency. A few tears were shed, but a large weight was lifted off my shoulders. Beyond discussing the why, we also talked about logical next steps. She offered her recommendation and wished me luck. We hugged, and I left her office quickly, hoping my tear-stained eyes wouldn't start the dispatch gossip train. News would be out soon enough, and at this point I didn't care. I had made my choice, and I was ready for the next chapter.

Lea

Beyond the pomp and circumstance of the wonderful "you are dead to us" cake and inside joke gifts, I had been dreading this day. Years later, remembering this day still makes my chest tighten. I dreaded it because I knew I would miss the job so much. I would miss the radio. The people. The work. The excitement. The rush. But on the other hand, I was so happy to be done going to work at eight o'clock at night. Done with the sleepless days and foggy brain, done with feeling like an absolute zombie and not being the mom and wife my family deserves. All of it. Done.

Despite this logical reasoning, my head and heart were heavy going into work for my final shifts. Somehow every fiber in my body knew these were my last radio transmissions and phone calls as a telecommunicator. In the days leading up to my last shift, I cried a lot. (News flash! I am an emotional person!) When faced with the finality of my decision, I knew it was going to be a hard night.

After packing the last items in my office and having a few laughs with my favorite deputies who came to see me off, I placed my headset atop my ear and clicked into the console for one last hoorah. I asked for Channel One, and my team, even Mallory, were happy to let me have it. I wanted one last ride on the bucking bronco that I had grown to love so much. With a lump in my throat, I cued up my first transmissions. I thought maybe patrol would make it interesting, but nothing of note occurred. Traffic stops, follow-ups, community business checks. All routine. It was a docile graveyard night—a real snooze fest. And the phone calls were even more mundane: a fallen victim at an assisted living facility, increases for neighborhood patrols, a request for an on-call victim advocate to speak with a deputy at our jail who was assaulted by an inmate.

This humdrum night left room for my favorite thing: socializing with my team, whom I had grown to truly love. That last night was filled with playing our favorite card game, Hand and Foot. I think I won? Either way, Mallory probably accused me of foul play.

When the night came to its inevitable end, my fellow kick-ass supervisor, who was also my mentor, best friend, and office partner, escorted me out of the building. She gave me a big hug, collected my badge, and told me she would see me soon. I didn't cry as I pulled out of the parking lot to race the dawn home and get into my bed. I knew I had made the right decision, and my heart was at peace.

My time wearing the headset was a mix of highs, lows, and everything between. While my eight years certainly came with trauma, I look back on the majority of it with sincere fondness. Reminiscing about my time as a telecommunicator is nostalgic, like walking into your childhood bedroom. I fondly remember the good times—the great times! Lots of potlucks, laughs, fun, baby showers, friendships, love, great card games, engaging training days, and success. I grew up at this job. It was the first time I received promotions and raises and experienced how hard work pays off. I grew my family at this job. I made lifelong friendships with amazing coworkers. I mourned the loss of my mother in that building. I was a part of programs that served my community and truly made a difference. Best job ever.

During the next month, a tornado of change blew through my life. We sold our house in three days. I packed the house in a fervor of commotion and carpal tunnel. One last family trip to the mountains and a pizza night in our empty foyer with friends and family punctuated three decades of living in Colorado. I seemingly blinked and woke up in a different state, with a new house and a new job. I stripped my life down to the bare bones, only to rebuild it better, stronger, and more powerful. I have no regrets. I know everything I did was God's will. I prayed, and He answered. He rescued. He provided. He reached into my brokenness and blessed me with promise and abundance. And for that, I am forever grateful.

I still miss the rush of dispatching a hot call or being in the thick of it when all hell breaks loose. I miss the gratification of working at the heartbeat of civil service. I miss my friends.

Some of my fondest memories come from those "Two for Tuesday" afternoons with Talia, where we'd enjoy back-to-back classic rock hits, soaking in the rhythm of our favorite bands while juggling calls. Laughter came easily in the center, like when we'd play back the radio traffic of Jordan unknowingly serenading the volunteer fire department with her open mic—moments that had us all in stitches.

But there were also quiet, somber times, like passing around that box of tissues during debriefs, when even the strongest among us—couldn't help but break on the toughest days. In between those highs and lows, we found joy in the little things, like the day I finally beat Geoff at his own guessing game during a training session, running around the table in gleeful victory. Or the time I was lovingly chastised for my "creative" recipe substitutions when tasked with bringing spinach artichoke dip—because, who knew mayonnaise couldn't be replaced?

There were countless card games, where we'd talk about work, life, and everything in between. But the greatest satisfaction came from watching trainees transform—not just into skilled telecommunicators, but into margarita-drinking friends and fellow warriors who braved the worst of every day alongside me. I faced storms, chaos, and uncertainty, yet through it all, I found strength and stride and enjoyed an incredible journey.

Perhaps that is one way to heal trauma: reflect more on the good times. I think that is good advice for anyone. In the darkness, remember your courage and, more importantly, your choice to focus on the light.

Now that you have consumed these stories, you have officially joined our club of twisted minds. Welcome to the dark side! Insert maniacal master villain laugh! In addition to proving to our husbands that people would read these stories, we wanted to serve a greater purpose. Do you think we chose to tell you these stories merely for cheap entertainment? Share them for your quick-read-while-sipping-a-Mai-Thai-in-Cancun-by-the-pool-fix? Bare some of the most intimate moments of our lives as something to gossip about with your friends? Thinking we are just trying to make a quick buck?

No. Definitely not. Why then?

Because Emma and I need your help. You have read something really valuable that could help change the 911 industry. Please recall our stories and interactions with 911 callers so that if you ever need to call 911, you will be prepared and have the best possible outcome. Even armed with this knowledge, you will be nervous! Remember Emma calling 911 three times during her 2021 summer "vacations"? She was nervous about each call—a 911 supervisor versed in all sorts of scary situations, experiencing trepidation to dial the three-digit number. If you ever find yourself in an emergency, these six tips will help you partner with the telecommunicator to have the best possible outcome.

1. **Do not call for anything that is not life-threatening.** If you have the time and mental capacity to google the nonemergency number during your "emergency" then you do NOT need to call 911. *Pro tip: prepare yourself by programming the nonemergency dispatch line for frequently traveled areas in your cell phone's favorites list.*

2. **Keep calm.** If possible, take a deep breath and speak as evenly as possible. Those who are calm communicate information better and get help faster than those who need to be talked off the ledge first. *If you call 911, take a deep breath and be prepared with a level head.*

3. **Know your location.** The first question the telecommunicator will ask is where you are located. Location matters more than what is

happening because *where* dictates which jurisdiction will respond. A telecommunicator MUST know where you are in order to send the right people. If you don't know it, be ready to grab a piece of mail, describe your settings, or use the tools around you to help the telecommunicator. *Be prepared with this information or equip yourself with an attitude to help, not fight, the process of location finding.*

4. **Follow directions.** Telecommunicators are the bossiest people in the world. They are trained to ask many questions in order to understand a situation from all angles and prepare first responders before they arrive on scene. This mission oftentimes includes giving very specific instructions and asking a lot of questions. Questions and instructions do not delay a response, so answer the questions and don't fight the information-gathering process. *Be prepared to help, not hinder a telecommunicator by following directions.*

5. **Do not hang up.** If you get frustrated by questions or transfers, hanging up makes the process longer. Every time you hang up, the telecommunicator has to spend precious seconds calling you back. If you don't answer, then more time and research goes into tracking you down! If you stay on the phone, help will more quickly arrive. *Be prepared to stay on the line for help.*

6. **Keep your devices updated.** As 911 services transition into a data-driven era, consider the impact on you. Evaluate the variety of devices you possess—watches, phones, sensors, and home alarm systems—all increasingly vital in life-saving scenarios thanks to technological advancements. It's crucial to ensure that your devices are outfitted with your current medical profiles and essential information. Keeping your profile updated on all your devices and researching personal emergency preparedness solutions for their connections to your local PSAP can be a literal lifesaver.

By following these tips, you can be ultra-prepared if you ever must call 911. We really hope you don't ever have to, but now you have some formal training about being effective and efficient in the event. Don't forget to share this with others, too!

On the other side of the phone, telecommunicators are fighting for classification with the National Labor Relations Board. Now that you have a very raw picture of what it is like to sit in the chair of a telecommunicator—not an easy chair to fill—you know that this job demands complex critical thinking ability, exceptional communication skills, and extreme multitasking requirements wrapped up with the ability to quickly respond and then recover from life-or-death interactions. The brave men and women on the other side of your 911 calls are heroes. They save lives. Chris Nussman aptly notes, "Sadly...the U.S. Bureau of Labor Statistics' Standard Occupational Classification Systems (SOCS) categorizes public safety telecommunicators. . .as 'Office and Administrative Support Occupations.'"[15] Yes, the US government views the person who could save your life or the life of a loved one as a secretary.

The good news and hope is that by supporting an active Congress bill called the Support Accurate Views of Emergency Services Act (911 SAVES Act), you can help make a difference. The passing of this monumental bill, reintroduced by Congress leadership in November 2023, would reclassify the public safety telecommunicator as a "Protective Service Occupation," alongside law enforcement personnel, firefighters, security guards, and others whose job it is to protect our communities.[16]

This change may seem insignificant, but it would give an estimated 100,000 public safety telecommunicators located in every community across America the support they deserve while improving the government's data collection and analysis efforts. The bill costs the taxpayers nothing and grants the telecommunicators recognition, visibility, funding, better pay, and access to healthcare benefits specially classified for those dealing with a mental health crisis or PTSD from job stress.

Now that you know what it is like in the 911 hot seat (our apologies for the emotional scars), we hope you can agree that telecommunicators are not secretaries. They are first responders and should be recognized thusly, nationwide. Join the fight to reclassify telecommunicators by sending support via the National Emergency Numbers Association (NENA) website [17] for the 911 SAVES Act.

Beyond the education and call to action, we hope this book is a conversation starter. Let's talk about seatbelt safety. Drinking and driving. Suicides. Domestic violence. America's mental health crisis. Let's open the door and let the light into the nooks and crannies that make us uncomfortable in order to forge paths to health, safety, and success.

Thank you for reading. Thank you for being a part of this journey. Thank you for educating yourself and others. We tip our telecommunicator headsets to you all!

Alert tone A high-pitched noise that a telecommunicator uses preceding the airing of an emergent call. The purpose of a tone is to get the attention of all first responders, so they do not miss the dispatch and have situational awareness.

AVL (Automatic Vehicle Locators) Software installed in first responder vehicles that allows for location information to be relayed to other first responders and telecommunicators to aide in tracking and dispatching nearby units for quicker response.

Bearcat A highly specialized armored vehicle that provides tactical protection in high-intensity law enforcement situations.

BOLO (Be on the Lookout) Communication shared between law enforcement agencies describing dangerous suspects or situations. The intent in sharing this information is to inform and prepare nearby jurisdictions about the possibility of similar encounters or to establish patterns.

CAD (Computer Aided Dispatch) A software program that allows telecommunicators within the PSAP to simultaneously create, update, and track calls for service.

Call for service An event taking place requiring first responder attention. This event can be an emergency or nonemergency situation.

Channel One (a.k.a., "Primary") The main radio channel a PSAP utilizes to communicate with first responders. Functionality includes assigning calls for service to first responders based on staffing, location, skill level, and equipment. Additionally, Channel One tracks first responder locations, airs updated information about calls for service, and assists field units with ancillary needs.

Channel Two (a.k.a., "Data Channel") A secondary radio channel a PSAP utilizes to communicate with first responders. Functionality includes calling for secondary responders like tow trucks, victim advocates, coroner, etc. Also used for clearing drivers, cars, and license plates. Data Channel additionally helps make entries into state/national warrant and records systems.

CIRT (Critical Incident Response Team) A team comprised of multiagency investigators who respond to officer-involved shootings to process the scene and conduct interviews. Their sole purpose is to objectively determine if the use of force by a first responder was warranted in the situation.

Code 3 (a.k.a., "lights and sirens") When a first responder proceeds to a call for service activating lights, sirens, and high speed as tools for faster response. Department policy and procedure dictate what situations justify a Code 3 response. Code 3 responses must be aired so that a ranking officer can approve or deny the action.

Code 4 A situational status first responders provide to indicate they are safe.

Command Line A prompt field in the CAD software used to execute updates and make changes to the calls for service via predetermined codes and sequences.

CPR (Cardiopulmonary Resuscitation) An emergency procedure that rhythmically rotates chest compressions and rescue breathing in an effort to keep blood circulating and brain function intact ahead of the arrival of first responders.

CSP (Colorado State Patrol) A law enforcement agency that specializes in traffic related incidents in the state of Colorado. They are the authority for highway-related calls for service. Local agencies regularly liaise with them for accident reports.

Dispo'd Describes the disposition or end of a call. Usually, dispo's are provided by officers or deputies. Common call dispositions are CR (Case Report), NR (No Report), UTL (Unable to Locate).

EMD (Emergency Medical Dispatch) A medical protocol system that telecommunicators use to give lifesaving instructions to callers on the phone ahead of the arrival of first responders.

Felony stop When an officer of the law initiates a traffic stop on a stolen vehicle. Once the vehicle is pulled over, the officer approaches the suspect vehicle with their gun drawn.

GSW Gunshot wound.

MetroNet A shared radio channel that connects agencies within close geographical proximity, allowing them share direct transmissions. Used in situations to save time and share pertinent information about emergency situations and suspects.

NCIC (National Crime Information Center) A nationwide classified database of information used to inform law enforcement about the criminal status of persons and articles. This database is accessed through secure terminals or computer stations subject to rigorous protection by those who endure lengthy training to interpret the data and use it without malice.

PSAP (Public Safety Answering Point) The location/center where emergency and nonemergency calls are answered.

Radio Traffic or "traffic" The communication between telecommunicators and first responders that happens on a selected radio channel. Radio transmissions are always recorded and fiercely monitored in line with Federal Communications Commission (FCC) standards.

RapidSOS Web-based intelligent safety platform that delivers data-rich information, such as caller location, health details, and crash detection, directly to 911 telecommunicators and first responders.

RP (Reporting Party) An emergency or nonemergency caller.

Safe2Tell A statewide program that allows for anonymous reporting of harmful events, persons, or situations within schools. Safe2Tell reports are funneled to local PSAPs and to school administrators for proper handling.

Select (or "turn up") When a telecommunicator clicks into a radio channel for monitoring.

SWAT (Special Weapons and Tactics) A highly trained and equipped police unit that responds and then resolves high-risk situations, including shootouts, standoffs, raids, hostage takings, and terrorism.

Thin Blue Line Police community.

Thin Gold Line Telecommunicator community.

Transmit or Transmission When a telecommunicator speaks on the radio to first responders. Transmissions are successfully executed by selecting into a radio channel and clicking the channel transmit button via the radio software, depressing the console foot pedal, or holding down the headset base radio button.

VA (Victim Advocate) A civilian member of a law enforcement agency provided to victims of crimes for helping to navigate their rights and next steps in the judicial process. Often these individuals are trained volunteers.

Acknowledgements

To our forever partners, best friends, and champions in all things: Spencer and Caleb. When we said we were going to do this crazy thing, you didn't bat an eye and allowed us to run with it full force. We asked for your advice, and you met us with respect, budgeting for this dream and supporting us through tears, writers block, and sister fights. The phrase "we couldn't have done it without you" is a gross understatement.

Also, immense thanks to our best supporting actors and actresses who turned this dream into reality: Brittany Rose, Tammy Klepac, and Hayley Smith. Brittany and Tammy, you not only styled us but also joined us in Hayley's charming bookshop and picturesque meadows. Together, we laughed and added a professional touch to this incredible journey with your outstanding photography skills.

To another creative master, Ty Nowicki. Your guidance, advice and ingenuity are driving forces for where we are today. From reading the initial few pages and making professional recommendations for logical next steps, to helping us form a solid title and creating a cover that encompasses our vision—you are a master of your craft and we are blessed because you shared your talent with us so graciously. Still not sure if it's because you are part of the family or not. . .Either way, you are a keeper!

Jennifer Hunt. When I met you in my kitchen with spinach dip (made with mayonnaise) and interruptions from a stubborn three-year-old negotiating bedtime, you accepted the challenge to edit this complex manuscript with bravery. Your focus singularly turned this brainchild from a series of diary entries to a full-fledged manuscript that recounts our years of service. Thank you for your time, dedication, and advice where we needed it most. Your skill with the red pen is supreme. Mom didn't get her chance to do it, but I'm glad God sent us you. Welcome to the family.

To those who repeatedly showed interest in these stories and our journeys, THANK YOU because you continually challenged us to keep going. We value you as supporters, friends, family, and now, readers.

[*] Many acronyms and vernacular are associated with this profession, so we added a glossary at the end of the book to help you. You are welcome!

Notes

[1] National Emergency Number Association (NENA) PSAP Operations Committee, 9-1-1 Call Processing Working Group, *NENA Standard for 9-1-1 Call Processing*, Alexandria, VA: NENA, 2020, https://cdn.ymaws.com/www.nena.org/resource/resmgr/standards/nena-sta-020.1-2020_911_call.pdf.

[2] "CPR Facts & Stats," American Heart Association, accessed July 18, 2022, https://cpr.heart.org/en/resources/cpr-facts-and-stats/.

[3] Amit K. Reddy et al, "Survivors of Self-inflicted Gunshot Wounds to the Head: Characterization of Ocular Injuries and Health Care Costs," *JAMA Ophthalmology* 132, no. 6 (June 2014): 730–736, https://doi.org/10.1001/jamaophthalmol.2013.8201.

[4] "Domestic Violence Statistics," National Domestic Violence Hotline, accessed July 18, 2022, https://www.thehotline.org/stakeholders/domestic-violence-statistics/.

[5] "Text-to-911," APCO International, accessed January 24, 2024, https://www.apcointl.org/technology/next-generation-9-1-1/text-to-911/.

[6] "PSAP Text-to-911 Readiness and Certification Registry (Text-to-911 Registry)," Federal Communications Commission, accessed January 24, 2024, https://www.fcc.gov/general/psap-text-911-readiness-and-certification-form.

[7] *New World Encyclopedia*, s.v. "Flow (psychology)," accessed August 20, 2022, https://www.newworldencyclopedia.org/entry/ Flow_(psychology).

[8] Josh McFadden, "Pocket Dialing," *The Journal of Emergency Dispatch*, February 23, 2016, https://www.iaedjournal.org/pocket-dialing.

[9] "Mental Health Disorder Statistics," Johns Hopkins Medicine, accessed January 24, 2024, https://www.hopkinsmedicine.org/health/wellness-and-prevention/mental-health-disorder-statistics.

[10] "Drowning Facts," Centers for Disease Control and Prevention, accessed January 24, 2024, https://www.cdc.gov/drowning/facts/index.html.

[11] Roger Michell, *Notting Hill* (1999; Universal City, CA: Universal Pictures, 1999), 4K Ultra HD Blu-ray Disc.

[12] Peter Jackson, *The Lord of the Rings: The Two Towers* (2002; Los Angeles, CA: New Line Cinema, 2003), 4K Ultra HD Blu-ray Disc.

[13] Peter Jackson, *The Lord of the Rings: The Two Towers* (2002; Los Angeles, CA: New Line Cinema, 2003), 4K Ultra HD Blu-ray Disc.

[14] "Rescue," Lauren Daigle, Spotify, track 2 on *Look Up Child*, Centricity Music, 2018.

[15] Chris Nussman, "911 SAVES Act Introduced: It's Time to Give 9-1-1 Pros the Respect They Deserve," *NENA: The 9-1-1 Association,*. April 1, 2021, https://www.nena.org/news/559127/

911-Saves-Act-Introduced-Its-Time-to-Give-9-1-1-Pros-the-Respect-They-Deserve.htm.

[16] https://www.congress.gov/bill/118th-congress/house-bill/6319/.

[17] https://www.votervoice.net/NENA/Campaigns/ 108990/Respond.

About the Author

Emma Lee was born and raised in Colorado. She is a current 911 telecommunication supervisor with over nine years of service. She has a bachelor's degree in clinical exercise science and a minor in sports psychology. She resides in the Northern Colorado region and is also a business owner. She is married to her best friend, and they have one son, who keeps her busy with school activities and sports. Emma's perfect day includes hitting the gym, hiking with her adventure dogs, and ending the day with a home-cooked meal joined by family and friends. If Emma could travel the world with her family forever, she would.

Lea Harms is a Colorado native, author, speaker, and retired 911 telecommunicator. Armed with her master's degree in communication studies, her work passions include project management and adult learning during dynamic changes. She now resides in Texas with her husband, two children, and loyal dogs. After working graveyard shifts for years, her biggest accomplishment these days is kissing her two sleeping babies before bed every night. In a busy season of mom duties, a perfect day involves swimming in the family pool, cruising to grandma's house blasting music, and ending the night cuddled on couches watching a movie. When this season changes, she hopes to return to her regularly scheduled programming, which includes traveling the world, watching any theatre production, and kicking butt on American Tough Mudder courses.

Read more at www.leaharms.com.